FACING THE UNTHINKABLE

Produced by Raymond Creed,
Director of *'Rebuild Christianity Publications'*

Author of: -

'The Fifty-Two Attributes of G-d'

'The Leeds Liturgy'

'The Phantom Conflict'

Storefront

http://stores.lulu.com/rebuildchristianity or

http://stores.lulu.com/store.php?fAcctID=976144

Copies of soft cover editions may also be available through Amazon and other International Distributors

FACING THE UNTHINKABLE

(How Israel will find the true Messiah)

Zechariah: 12:10b
"And they shall mourn for Him as one mourns for his only son"

Thought Starter
To gain true faith in the Lord we must lose faith in ourselves and in our own capacity to please Him

Raymond Creed

Copyright © the Author 2010
(Backdated to cover all material and versions produced by the author prior to 2010)

All Rights Reserved,
The *'Moral Right'* of the author has been asserted.

First (Pilot) Edition 1998, limited distribution only to family and friends, is now out of print

Second (Trial Book) Edition 2008, wasn't available for international distribution is now out of print

Third (International) Edition 2010, should be available through international distributors like Amazon

Fourth (Electronic edition) 2017 should be available on Amazon Kindle

Fifth Licensed Edition 2019

ISBN: 978-1-907910-01-2

The name of the Deity has been abbreviated to *'G-d'* out of respect for Jewish religious sensitivities that regard the divine name as being too holy to pronounce.

Contents

Introduction	VIII
Preface: An Air of Mystery	IX
Update	XI
License	XIII
THE *'RESCUE OF ISRAEL'* LITURGY	**1**
Dedication	3
Prologue: The Nations Rage	4
A: Confessional and *'Calling'* Sections	**5**
Section 1: The Return 1-18	7
Section 2: The Confession of Sin 1-34	15
Section 3: The *'Calling'* 1-19	24
B: The *'Coming to Faith'* Sections	**33**
Section 4: The Invocation 1-17	35
Section 5: The Recognition 1-5	42
Section 6: How Could We? 1-5	44
C: Praise and Pleading Sections	**47**
Section 7: Messianic Praise 1-10	49
Section 8: Pleading for the Messiah's Return 1-11	50
Section 9: Rejoice, Oh Israel 1-10	54
D: Closing Section	**59**
Section 10: Fulfilment 1-14	61
Appendices	**63**
Appendix 1: Saul of Tarsus: The Forerunner of Israel	65

Appendix 2: The Witness ... 68

Appendix 3: What Is Midrash? ... 81

Selective Bibliography ... **103**

Book List ... 105

Articles ... 107

Reference Works ... 108

Media Sources ... 108

Various Source ... 108

Other Titles by the Author ... **109**

The 52 Attributes of G-d ... 111

The Leeds Liturgy ... 112

The Phantom Conflict ... 114

Titles in Preparation ... **115**

Ancient Hatred ... 117

Ancient Love ... 118

Key to Symbols

All: Congregation and leaders

P1: Presiding Participant

P2: Other participants in worship

P1-2: Presiding Participant is to alternate with other participants

M: The Messiah

N: Name of person or situation needing prayer

Q: Questioning Individual

Any wording within square brackets [ ] represents anyone of the following: -

1. An optional section of the liturgy, which may be omitted (should time be limited)

2. Alternative wording, used to provide variety between different worship sessions

3. An amplification of a given Bible passage

Introduction

Facing the Unthinkable dramatically portrays the likely spiritual, emotional and psychological reactions of a beleaguered number of Jewish people at the very point when they turn to their true Messiah. Their state of near-total despair will suddenly change to one of exuberant joy. Following their recognition and acceptance of the Messiah all the bible prophecies concerning the restoration of Israel will begin to be fulfilled. This book breaks new ground in its creative expression and by its use of different literary forms to convey key points. Readers are given a vivid sense of what it's like to receive an overwhelming revelation of divine love.

'Facing the Unthinkable' provides hope for the Messianic Jewish Community and for those Christians with a genuine interest in the Jewish people. It helps rebuild Christianity by emphasising its links to both Israel and Judaism. Great care is taken to address the following questions: -
1) How will the Jewish people come to believe in their true Messiah?
2) How will they react when they encounter Him?
3) How will the world react to this unexpected development?

It's assumed that both the nation of Israel and the whole of humanity itself will be on the brink of annihilation before this unique event happens. G-d will have allowed much suffering to have taken place to highlight Man's abject failure in his attempt to create a *'New World Order.'* The promise of a better and fairer world (made by a false global messiah) will have been cruelly exposed and falsified.

'Facing the Unthinkable' is an invaluable resource for Messianic Jews and those engaged in any form of Jewish work or those having a sympathetic interest in the State of Israel. It may be regarded as an independent publication or as a companion work to 'The Leeds Liturgy.'

Readers who don't wish to know *how* 'Facing the Unthinkable' was built-up over a long-time period should skip the preface and proceed to 'The License' on XII or 'The Rescue of Israel Liturgy' on p.1.

To purchase a download, hard or soft cover edition, please visit: -

http://stores.lulu.com/rebuildchristianity or

http://stores.lulu.com/store.php?fAcctID=976144

Soft cover editions are also available through Amazon and other International Distributors.

Preface: An Air of Mystery

An air of mystery surrounds *'The Rescue of Israel Liturgy'*[1] simply because its actual goal has, yet, to be realised. Whether it will be followed *'word for word'* remains to be seen. What it does do is to anticipate the strong emotions that many Jewish people may feel at the time of Israel's public recognition of the Messiah. Present will be a movement from near total despair to sudden and exuberant joy. The Liturgy itself adheres closely to scripture in its assumption that both Israel and humankind will be on the brink of annihilation before this recognition takes place. Israel's public recognition of Yeshua will occur amidst a global holocaust – this tragedy having been allowed by the Almighty to break human resistance to His divine will. Reinforcing this point is the prophecy of Joel 2:27f which reveals that the Holy Spirit will be poured out on Israel at a time of *"blood, fire and pillars of smoke,"* (Joel 2:30b). Looming over the glorious promise of revival is the spectre of the mushroom cloud. Hardly surprisingly, many who preach from this passage often overlook this aspect. Also, the outpouring of the Spirit at Pentecost (Acts 2) represented only an initial fulfilment of the promise made earlier in Joel 2:27f. A more encompassing fulfilment will take place nearer Christ's Second Coming and will be directed towards the surviving *'remnant of Israel'* as mentioned in Zechariah 13:8-9.

The spiritual link existing between the Nation of Israel and a true Church of remnant believers means there is every reason to suppose that this fulfilment of the outpouring of G-d's Spirit will apply to those gentile believers living at that pivotal moment in history (when Israel will publicly recognise the true Messiah). Like the Jews, they too will need an outpouring of the Holy Spirit to face the dreadful hardship they will be called upon to endure. Hence, this outpouring will be bestowed *'upon all flesh'* – meaning believers in all nations (Joel 2:28b) as well as upon the small remnant of Jews. However, this book is intended mainly for the *'remnant of Israel'* and represents the writer's legacy to the Jewish people. Up to and including **Section 5,** it is assumed that those who use it are not yet true believers in the Messiah although they may be earnestly seeking divine intervention to be rescued from destruction. Divine intervention will come in the end, but only on G-d's terms. In the meantime, it's hoped that those who are already true believers in the Messiah will be both edified and challenged. At the very least, they should gain some idea as to what the Jews will be feeling when *'the scales'* drop from their eyes. The full significance of this liturgy will most probably only be acknowledged with the passing of the years. Although a great deal of time has been spent in putting this work together, the

---

[1] Most of this Liturgy was first drafted in handwritten form during March 1997, but extensive use was made of earlier material. It was originally entitled, *'The Remnant of Israel Liturgy.'*

writer still feels that he's barely scratched the surface of a truly great mystery. Paul's own revelation on the Damascus Road perhaps anticipated a more widespread revelation to be given to Israel at a future date[2] – however, only time and circumstances will reveal more.

Nonetheless, as a *'rule of thumb'* it really is poor marketing practice to openly admit to having scarcely any idea at all as to why a work was written in the first place. Such an admission would generate a rejection slip from any publisher. Moreover, the writer's more usual approach has been to draw up a detailed list of *'aims'* and *'objectives'* before embarking upon any literary project. However, since this material was first word processed in the summer and early autumn of 1998 it has become increasingly apparent that another attempt to destroy the Jewish people is now in the making and the Western World has itself become complicit in such an attempt.[3] It may well prove to be the case that a surviving remnant of Jewish people will feel the need to refer to this book to facilitate their return to G-d. Through it they should be encouraged to interact with scripture in a deep and personal way.

Readers may notice some differences between *'The Leeds Liturgy'* and this work. One such difference is that of tone; where most sections of *'The Leeds Liturgy'* adopt either a soberly didactic or worshipful tone, this document moves quickly from bleak desperation to ecstatic joy. It has the capacity to express very strong emotions. One reason for this contrast lies in the purpose of each separate work. *'The Leeds Liturgy'* is designed for the regular life of G-d's people, with its main emphasis upon the intelligent worship of G-d through the recitation of Creeds and other devotional material (with most culminating in the Lord's Supper). The intention is to offer a broad overview of Biblical truth to reduce the risk of any unbalanced sectarianism (which occurs when over-zealous groups mistake one aspect of divinely revealed truth for the whole). Designed for regular use, its natural location can range from the local congregation to the large cathedral – although domestic use in the privacy of one's home is also envisaged. *'The Leeds Liturgy'* has a target market consisting of those who are already regenerate believers in Jesus Christ. Its key role is to deepen a faith which is already there.

In contrast, *'The Rescue of Israel'* Liturgy is designed to meet a specific crisis facing the Jewish people. The intention is to facilitate their recognition of the true Messiah and to help them express the very diverse feelings they may well experience as a direct result of that event. Consequently, it focuses upon a far narrower range of Biblical

---

[2] Appendix 1 *'Saul: Forerunner of Israel'* was inserted on Thursday, 28th August 2003 because Paul's recognition of Jesus as the Messiah was anticipating that of his own people in a future time

[3] Detailed documentation in support of this point is provided by Melanie Phillips in her book *'The World Turned Upside Down.'*

teaching, but with a far greater set of (often lengthy) quoted Bible passages. The natural setting of this publication is the besieged city or battlefield dugout with its intended audience consisting mainly of a beleaguered remnant of Jewish people on the brink of destruction. Driven to desperation, they will be in a position where they will feel almost forced to begin seeking the truth. *'The Rescue of Israel Liturgy'* charts their move from unbelief to belief. It lays bare the sometimes messy psychological and spiritual processes involved in a sudden, drastic change of religious belief. Vividly conveyed is the feeling of raw shock arising from the discovery that one's whole life has been based upon incorrect assumptions about G-d and human nature. For Jewish people at the time, it will appear as if their entire world has been turned upside down. This liturgy will begin to be used at that specific future point in time when a remnant of Jewish people really will recognise the Messiah. It is envisaged that it will be used for subsequent anniversaries of that same event. It really is a Liturgy for a special event and for commemorative occasions thereafter.

For now (November 2010), public interest in both this work and the *'Leeds Liturgy'* is minimal. The writer is heartily glad that he's not in the business of trying to write best sellers – least of all in theology where the only books with a high sales volume are usually heretical. There is the added complication that theology is an increasingly marginalised subject, enjoying little status in the world of academia or elsewhere. Sadly, it has become a plaything for aloof academics or zealous fanatics. As a coherent discipline, theology has lost sight of its central goal, which is <u>to help people to know and love G-d</u> or at least to help them know and love Him better. Without this priority, theology becomes nothing more than an intellectual game, tending only to confuse rather than enlighten. It has lost any credibility in the wider society. Both the *'Leeds'* and *'Rescue of Israel'* Liturgies attempt to recall theology to its priority by re-connecting truth with worship. An interactive approach is followed because it's recognized that the result of all good theology should not be endless debate but endless praise.

What the writer refuses to do is to *'dumb down.'* He is <u>not</u> in the business of writing material that could be entitled *'worship for dummies.'* Rather, the intention is to produce well-crafted literature, which should prove of lasting benefit to both Jewish and non-Jewish believers. Adopted is the principle of *'supply economics,'* which states *'first supply the goods and then the demand will eventually follow.'* A comparison can be made with a motorway network – the motorways had first to be built before vehicles could travel on them. His strategy is to produce the material, alert relevant market niches to this fact and then allow G-d to create the demand in His own way and time. Although this may sound rather *'holier than thou'* it appears to be the only sensible strategy to follow. Large numbers of people will come to use these Liturgies only when events create a need for them. The increasing likelihood of a war of extermination in the Middle East and other world developments (like the growing threat to the environment) suggest that such a need could build up very quickly in all kinds of unexpected places.

In the meantime, it is the writer's hope that, in His gracious mercy, the Lord G-d of Israel will use this Liturgy to help His Jewish people to recognise His Son Jesus as their true Messiah.[4]

The Author: Thursday, 9th December 2010

Update: Friday, 7th July 2017

Towards the end of 2016, a rapid deterioration in the World's Political Situation (as exemplified by the vitriolic American Presidential Election of that year) obliged me to consider whether I should adopt a more proactive approach in distributing *'Facing the Unthinkable.'* Initially, I was reluctant to follow this option as I was busy fulfilling a variety of demanding literary and professional commitments. Consequently, it was only during a personal prayer retreat (held in January 2017) that the decision was made to cautiously proceed with this venture. Initially, the intention was not to do anything active until the summer of 2018. My feeling was that I had more than enough projects to complete during the interim. However, a threat to future financial security plus growing political instability and terrorist outrages in the United Kingdom forced my hand. I was persuaded to bring things forward to this summer. Present was an ambition to leave a worthwhile legacy that will bless the Jewish people. May God honour this endeavour, (Genesis 12:3a).

A decisive moment came on Good Friday, 14th April, whilst visiting Jerusalem with my eldest and youngest sons. (This was when both the Christian Festival of Easter and the Jewish Passover were underway.) On that day, surrounded by chanting Jewish men, I stood against The Wailing Wall, quietly praying that God would *'use me to facilitate Israel's recognition of the Messiah.'* I was hoping to achieve this by acting as a resource provider – freely offering literature Jewish people could use during a time of great suffering when they will need to call upon the Lord to rescue them from total annihilation, (Joel 3:32 & Zechariah 13:8-9). To be used in this way would fulfil a lifetime's ambition. It would also give me scope to apply the instruction given in Isaiah 40:3b which reads, *"Prepare the way of the Lord, make straight in the desert a highway for our God."* With God's help, this is precisely what I've set out to accomplish through the production and distribution of this work.

---

[4] Appendix 2 *'The Witness'* was inserted on Monday 5th March 2007, the writer wishing to provide a <u>sensitive</u> Gospel witness to Jewish people

License

Under the terms of this license the author grants members of Messianic Jewish Congregations, Education Providers and those Ministries permanently based in Israel full permission to: -

A. Translate into Hebrew, Arabic, Russian and the Ethiopian languages of Amharic and Tigrinya this edition of *'Facing the Unthinkable.'*

B. To replicate and distribute electronic and non-electronic copies of this work for a profit of up to 10% on condition that: -

1. The distribution of non-electronic, hard and soft cover copies is confined within the State of Israel

2. The original source is acknowledged

3. No alteration is made to the contents.

4. At least one copy of those books listed under *'Other Titles'* is purchased

5. It is acknowledged that Copyright remains wholly with the original author.

6. No other copyright is placed upon any translated, replicated or distributed version

7. No contact takes place with the writer (or those closely associated with him) requesting money, material goods, banking details or help in gaining access to the United Kingdom or any other country.

8. It is accepted that the author is not financially, morally, legally (or in any other way) responsible for: -

- Damage, disturbance, harm or loss incurred by the above activities
- The financial affairs, legal disputes, teachings or conduct of those engaging in the above activities

It will be assumed that those parties engaged in the translation, replication and distribution of this work have given their willing consent to each of the above terms and conditions. Those in contravention of them will have this license withdrawn. The above license does not apply to any English version of this document (which will continue to be sold on a normal commercial basis).

XIV

THE RESCUE OF ISRAEL LITURGY

(A liturgy revealing the strong emotions which may well be felt by the Jewish people in Israel when, on the very precipice of annihilation, they recognise their true Messiah)

Raymond Creed

Zechariah 13:9
"And I will bring the third part [of Israel] through the fire and will refine them as silver is refined and will try them as gold is tried: they shall call on my name and I will hear them: I will say, 'it is my people' and they shall say, 'The Lord is my G-d.'"

Thought Starter
"One of the greatest events in history will be the recognition by the Jewish people of Jesus Christ as their Messiah"[5]

---

[5] An oft-repeated comment made by the writer's father in private conversation with the writer during the 1960s until 1990s

Editorial Note

This document was: -

First drafted, July-October 1998

Released onto the Internet in April 2003

Re-titled, January 2007

Revised, February-December 2007

Prepared for publication in book form January-March 2008 with corrections being made in October 2009 and in March 2010

Amended in October-November 2010 before being released for International Publication

Final Amendments June 2017 before being released for electronic distribution

Copyright © the Author 2010

All Rights Reserved, the Moral Right of the Author has been asserted but please see *'License'* for further details.

Dedication

This document is dedicated to my father (1914-1999) who first taught me to love the Jewish people and to envisage a great destiny for them; may his name be forevermore remembered in Israel.

This document is dedicated to my father (1914-1999) who first taught me to love the Jewish people and to envisage a great destiny for them; may his name be forevermore remembered in Israel.

Also to my mother (1923-2018) who even in extreme old age was an inspiration.

Finally, to my London-based maternal ancestors and their relatives in the Myerson line who during the nineteenth century came to know the Lord and serve Him faithfully.

May all the above rejoice in this work for the G-d we follow *"is not the God of the dead, but the God of the living,"* (Mark 12:27)

Prologue: The Nations Rage[6]

Like boiling water in a pan
The nations bubble
The nations rage
The nations seethe
The nations writhe

Yes, the nations are in turmoil
For they have all turned against G-d's people
In Israel
An irrational hatred guides their every action
They are united in a global rebellion
Against the Lord who created them

But like criminals sentenced to the gallows
Their destruction is near
The punishment of these nations cannot be deferred
Their time has run out
Their executioner awaits
Soon he will act

Armed masses gather in the land
Amidst the din of battle
Mighty military hordes struggle
No mercy is shown
Clouds of choking dust cover the scene

The noise of war is heard far away
Its clamour resounds in every nation
The world watches in suspense
Many pray to their various G-ds
But the annihilation of false religion draws near

In an instance of time
G-d will save His chosen ones
Many will perish
But those who remain
Will be a testimony to the entire world
For He is faithful to His covenant promises
Once made to Abraham

---

[6] Originally entitled *'The Nations Hiss'*, this poem was written on Friday, 24th January 1992 and emphasises how the Lord will rescue a remnant of Jewish people in Israel. This will take place during a time of armed conflict when each of the world's nations will be arrayed against them, (Psalm 2:1 & Zechariah 14:2). On Friday, 8th October 2010 its title was altered in response to comments made by friends and a family member.

A: CONFESSIONAL AND *'CALLING'* SECTIONS

6

Section 1: The Return

1) P1: *"Come let us return to the Lord; for He has torn* [us so that] *He will heal us; He has smitten* [us so that] *He will bind us up,"* (Hosea 6:1)

2) P2: *"After two days He will revive us; on the third day, He will raise us up and we shall live in His sight,"* (Hosea 6:2)

3) P1: *"Let us be zealous to follow the Lord;* [for] *his going forth is prepared as the morning; and He shall come unto us as the rain, as the latter* [autumnal) *and former* [spring-time] *rain unto the earth,"* (Hosea 6:3)

Pause

4) P1: As *"the congregation of Israel,"* (Exodus 12:6b) let us renew our faith by saying...

5) All: *"Hear! Oh, Israel the Lord our G-d is one Lord"*

6) P1: Let us remember the words G-d spoke to Moses on the Holy Mount when He commanded, *"You shall have no other G-ds before* [but] *me"* (Exodus 20:3)

7) P2: For He is the Lord who is *"a jealous G-d, visiting the iniquity of the fathers upon the children unto the third and fourth generation of them that hate,"* [Him] (Exodus 20:5b)

8) P1: Let us, in humble solemnity [seriousness], listen to the testimony of Moses who clearly warned against the consequences of disobeying divine Torah.

9) P2: Lord, grant us the courage to face searching questions and to discover why, despite all our great ethical and spiritual traditions, we seem to be under the most fearsome curses of the Law. Truly, your own Word testifies against us.

Begin first reading

In this and subsequent readings the Presiding Participant may: -
1. Personally read the passages aloud
2. Deputize someone with a clear, audible voice to perform this task
3. Read the odd numbered verses with the remainder of the group reading the even numbered verses.
4. Direct the congregation to read aloud all the verses
Each text should be read in a lucid and ready to understand manner with a brief pause following each passage.

Deuteronomy 28:15-67

15. But it shall come to pass, if you will not hearken unto the voice of the Lord your G-d, to observe to do all his commandments and his statutes which I command you this day; that all these curses shall come upon you and overtake you:

16. Cursed shall you be in the city and cursed shall you be in the field

17. Cursed shall be your basket and your store.

18. Cursed shall be the fruit of your body and the fruit of your land, the increase of your cattle and the flocks of your sheep

19. Cursed shall you be when you come in and cursed shall you be when you go out.

20. The Lord shall send upon you cursing, vexation and rebuke, in all that you set your hand to do, until you are destroyed and until you perish quickly; because of the wickedness of your doings, whereby you have forsaken me.

21. The Lord shall make the pestilence cleave unto you until he has consumed you from off the land whither you go to possess it.

22. The Lord shall smite you with consumption and with a fever and with an inflammation and with an extreme burning and with the sword and with blasting and with mildew; and they shall pursue you until you perish.

23. And your heaven that is over your head shall be brass and the earth that is under you shall be iron.

24. The Lord shall make the rain of your land powder and dust: from heaven shall it come down upon you, until you are destroyed.

25. The Lord shall cause you to be smitten before your enemies: you shall go out one way against them and flee seven ways before them: and shall be removed into all the kingdoms of the earth.

26. And your carcase shall be meat unto all fowls of the air and unto the beasts of the earth and no man shall be there to frighten them away.

27. The Lord will smite you with the boils of Egypt and with the tumours and with the scab and with the itch, which cannot be healed.

28. The Lord shall smite you with madness and blindness and astonishment of heart

29. And you shall grope at noonday, as the blind grope in darkness and you shall not prosper in your ways: and you shall be only oppressed and spoiled evermore and no man shall save you.

30. You shall betroth a wife and another man shall lie with her: you shall build a house and you shall not dwell therein: you shall plant a vineyard and shall not gather the grapes thereof.

31. Your ox shall be slain before your eyes and you shall not eat thereof: your ass shall be violently taken away from before your face and shall not be restored to you: your sheep shall be given unto your enemies and you shall have none to rescue them.

32. Your sons and your daughters shall be given unto another people and your eyes shall look and fail with longing for them all the daylong; and there shall be no might in your hand.

33. The fruit of your land and all your labours, shall a nation, which you know not, eat up and you shall be only oppressed and crushed always:

34. So that you shall be driven mad by what you shall see with the sight of your eyes.

35. The Lord shall smite you in the knees and in the legs, with sore boils that cannot be healed, from the sole of your foot unto the top of your head.

36. The Lord shall bring you and your king which you shall set over you, unto a nation which neither you nor your fathers have known; and there shall you serve other G-ds, wood and stone.

37. And you shall become [an object of] astonishment, a proverb and a byword among all nations whither the Lord shall lead you.

38. You shall carry much seed out into the field and shall gather but little in; for the locust shall consume it.

39. You shall plant vineyards and dress them, but shall neither drink of the wine, nor gather the grapes; for the worms shall eat them.

40. You shall have olive trees throughout all your coasts, but you shall not anoint yourself with the oil; for your olive shall cast its fruit.

41. *You shall beget sons and daughters, but you shall not enjoy them; for they shall go into captivity.*

42. *All your trees and the fruit of your land shall the locust consume.*

43. *The stranger that is within you shall get up above you very high; and you shall come down very low.*

44. *He shall lend to you and you shall not lend to him: he shall be the head and you shall be the tail.*

45. *Moreover all these curses shall come upon you and shall pursue you and overtake you, till you are destroyed; because you hearkened not unto the voice of the Lord your G-d, to keep his commandments and his statutes, which he commanded you:*

46. *And they shall be upon you for a sign and for a wonder and upon your seed.*

47. *Because you served not the Lord your G-d with joyfulness and with gladness of heart, for the abundance of all things;*

48. *Therefore shall you serve your enemies which the Lord shall send against you, in hunger and in thirst and in nakedness and in want of all things: and he shall put a yoke of iron upon your neck, until he has destroyed you!*

49. *The Lord shall bring a nation against you from far, from the end of the earth, as swift as the eagle flies; a nation whose tongue you shall not understand;*

50. *A nation of fierce countenance, which shall not regard the person of the old, nor show favour to the young:*

51. *And he shall eat the fruit of your cattle and the fruit of your land, until you are destroyed: which also shall not leave you corn, wine, or oil, or the increase of your cattle, or flocks of your sheep, until he has destroyed you.*

52. *And he shall besiege you in all your gates, until your high and fenced walls come down, which you trusted, throughout all your land: and he shall besiege you in all your gates throughout all your land, which the Lord your G-d has given you.*

53. *And you shall eat the fruit of your own body, the flesh of your sons and of your daughters, which the Lord your G-d has given you, in the siege and in the famished misery, wherewith your enemies shall distress you:*

54. *So that the man that is tender among you and very delicate, his eye shall be evil toward his brother and toward the wife of his bosom and toward the remnant of his children, which he shall leave:*

55. *So, that he will not give to any of them of the flesh of his children whom he shall eat: because he has nothing left him in the siege and in the famished misery, wherewith your enemies shall distress you in all your gates.*

56. *The tender and delicate woman among you, who would not adventure to set the sole of her foot upon the ground for delicateness and tenderness; her eye shall be evil toward the husband of her bosom and toward her son and toward her daughter,*

57. *And toward her young one that comes out from between her feet and toward her children whom she shall bear: for she shall eat them for want of all things secretly in the siege and famished misery, wherewith your enemy shall distress you in your gates.*

58. *If you will not observe to do all the words of this law that are written in this book, that you may fear this glorious and fearful name, THE LORD YOUR G-D;*

59. *Then the Lord will make your plagues wonderful and the plagues of your seed, even great, long-lasting plagues and sore long-lasting sicknesses.*

60. *Moreover he will bring upon you all the diseases of Egypt, which you were afraid of; and they shall cleave unto you.*

61. *Also every sickness and every plague, which is not written in the book of this law, them will the Lord bring upon you, until you be destroyed.*

62. *You shall be left few in number, whereas you were as the stars of heaven for multitude; because you would not obey the voice of the Lord your G-d*

63. *And it shall come to pass, that as the Lord rejoiced over you to do you good and to multiply you; so, the Lord will rejoice over you to* destroy you and to bring you to nothing; and you shall be plucked from off the land whither you go to possess it.

64. And the Lord shall scatter you among all people, from the one end of the earth even unto the other; and there you shall serve other G-ds, which neither you nor your fathers have known, even wood and stone.

65. And among these nations shall you find no ease, neither shall the sole of your foot have rest: but the Lord shall give you there a trembling heart and failing of eyes and sorrow of mind:

66. And your life shall hang in doubt before you; and you shall fear day and night and shall have no assurance of your life:

67. In the morning you shall say, 'Would G-d it was evening!' And at evening you shall say, 'Would G-d it was morning!' For you shall fear what you see with the sight of your eyes.

Pause: to allow people time to realise the extent to which the Mosaic curses are being applied

10) P1: Have not these curses come true, both in our history and at the present time?

11) P2: Yes, they have!

12) P1: Are not these curses coming true today in our Nation?

13) P2: Yes, they are!

14) P1: Do we not, for the sake of our families and loved ones have a responsibility to discover why these curses keep on happening?

15) P2: Yes, we do!

16) P1: Moreover, in this hour of destruction, do we not also have a responsibility to confess our sins in obedience to the Law of Moses? (Numbers 5:5:5-7)

17) P2: Yes, we do!

18) P1: Then let us bring our sins before G-d, trusting that, as with Abraham of old, G-d will provide His way of Atonement [covering of sin] (Genesis 22:1-17)

Begin second reading

Psalm 51

1. Have mercy upon me, oh G-d, according to your loving kindness: according to the multitude of your tender mercies blot out my transgressions.

2. Wash me thoroughly from mine iniquity and cleanse me from my sin.

3. For I acknowledge my transgressions: and my sin is ever before me.

4. Against you, you only, have I sinned and done this evil in your sight: that you might be justified when you speak and be clear when you judge.

5. Behold, I was shaped in iniquity; and in sin did my mother conceive me.

6. Behold, you desire truth in the inward parts: and in the hidden part you shall make me know wisdom.

7. Purge me with hyssop and I shall be clean: wash me and I shall be whiter than snow.

8. Make me hear joy and gladness; that the bones, which you have broken may rejoice.

9. Hide your face from my sins and blot out all my iniquities.

10. Create in me a clean heart, oh G-d; and renew a right spirit within me.

11. Cast me not away from your presence; and take not your holy spirit from me.

12. Restore unto me the joy of your salvation; and uphold me with your free spirit.

13. Then will I teach transgressors your ways; and sinners shall be converted unto you.

14. Deliver me from bloodguilt, oh G-d for you are the G-d of my salvation: and my tongue shall sing aloud of your righteousness.

15. Oh Lord, open my lips; and my mouth shall show forth your praise.

16. *For you desire not sacrifice else would I give it: you delight not in burnt offering.*

17. *The sacrifices of G-d are a broken spirit: a broken and a contrite heart, oh G-d, you will not despise.*

18. *Do good in your good pleasure unto Zion: build the walls of Jerusalem.*

19. *Then shall you be pleased with the sacrifices of righteousness, with burnt offering and whole burnt offering: then shall they offer bullocks upon your altar.*

Section 2: The Confession of Sin

1) P1: As we enter this time of confession and of bringing our situation before the Lord let us hear the testimony of our <u>first</u> witness, Moses, who said, (Deuteronomy 19:15),

2) All: *"You have sinned against the Lord and be sure your sin will find you out,"* (Numbers 32:23b)

3) P1: As our <u>second</u> witness let us hear the testimony of David, who said,

4) All: *"There is none that does good [we] have all gone aside, [we] are <u>all</u> together become filthy. There is not one who does good, no, <u>not</u> one,"* (Psalm 14:1c & 3)

5) P1: As our <u>third</u> witness let us hear the testimony of Isaiah, who said,

6) All: *"We are all as an unclean thing and our [self-] righteousness [is like] filthy rags covering the infected sores of lepers; we all do fade away as a leaf; and our iniquities, like the wind have taken us away,"* (Isaiah 64:6)

7) P1: *"You have hidden your face from us and have consumed us because of our iniquities,"* (Isaiah 64:7)

8) P2: *"Truly, our transgressions and sins are upon us and we waste away because of them,"* (Ezekiel 33:10b)

9) P1: As unrighteous sinners, let us now plead for the mercy of G-d

10) P2: *"But now Father, you are our Father. We are the clay and you are our potter; and we are all the work of your hand,"* (Isaiah 64:8)

11) P1: *"Be not very wrathful Oh Lord; do not remember our iniquity forever. Behold, we beseech you. See! We are all your people,"* (Isaiah 64:9)

12) P2: *"Your holy cities are a wilderness, Zion is a wilderness, Jerusalem a desolation,"* (Isaiah 64:10)

13) P1: *"Our holy and our beautiful house, where our fathers praised you is burned up with fire; and all our pleasant things are laid waste,"* (Isaiah 64:11)

14) P2: *"Will you restrain yourself for these things, Oh Lord? Will you hold your peace and afflict us very sorely?"* (Isaiah 64:12)

15) P1: Let us, with the strength given to us, mourn for our own personal sins of thought, word and deed, (Amos 9:5)

Pause: to allow time for personal confession to take place

16) P1: Let us look away from ourselves and mourn for those who have been killed or who have handed themselves over to Satanic deceit, by collaborating with our enemies, (Lamentations 5:15)

Pause

17) P1: Let us mourn for the Nation of Israel

Pause

18) P2: Let us mourn for all who are suffering and dying across the entire World

Pause

19) P1: Let us mourn for all the suffering of G-d's creatures in this time of disaster

Pause

20) P1: Now let us face reality and consider how, as individuals and as one nation of twelve tribes,[7] we fall hopelessly short of perfectly obeying the Commandments of Holy Torah

Begin third reading

The Ten Commandments

1. "You shall have no other G-ds but me
2. You shall not make any graven image or any likeness of anything that is in heaven above, or that is in the earth beneath, or that is in the waters beneath the earth. You shall not bow yourself [nor genuflect] to them; for I the Lord your G-d am a jealous G-d, visiting the iniquity of the fathers upon the children unto the third and fourth generation of them that hate me. And showing mercy unto thousands of them that love me and keep my commandments
3. You shall not take the name of the Lord your G-d in vain; for the Lord will not hold him guiltless who takes His name in vain.
4. Keep the Sabbath day to sanctify it, as the Lord your G-d has commanded you. Six days you shall labour and do all your work: But

---

[7] The myth that ten of the twelve tribes of Israel are lost is explicitly denied here.

the seventh day is the Sabbath of the Lord your G-d: in it you shall not do any work, neither you nor your son, nor your daughter, nor your manservant, nor your maidservant, nor your ox, nor your ass, nor any of the cattle, nor the stranger that is within your gates that your manservant and maidservant may rest as well as you. And remember that you were a slave in the land of Egypt and that the Lord your G-d brought you out through a mighty hand and by a stretched-out arm: therefore, the Lord your G-d commands you to keep the Sabbath day.
5. Honour your father and your mother, as the Lord your G-d has commanded you: that your days may be prolonged and that it may go well with you in the land, which the Lord G-d gives you
6. You shall not kill
7. Neither shall you commit adultery
8. Neither shall you steal
9. Neither shall you bear false witness against your neighbour
10. Neither shall you desire your neighbour's wife; neither shall you covet your neighbour's house, his field, or his manservant, or his maidservant, his ox, or his ass, or anything that is your neighbour's" (Exodus 20:2-17)

Pause

21) P1: *"These are the Commandments which the Lord commanded Moses for the children of Israel on Mount Sinai,"* (Leviticus 27:34). To obey these commandments in a way that pleases the Lord we must

22) All: *"Love the Lord* [our] G-d *with all [our] heart and with all* [our] *might"* (Deuteronomy 6:5) *"And love our neighbours as"* [ourselves.] (Leviticus19:18b).

23) P1: Lord, in all your ordinances we fall short of obeying your perfect will

24) P2: *"Have mercy upon us"* (Psalm 4:1)

25) P1: *"Have mercy upon* [us] *for* [we] *are desolate and afflicted,"* (Psalm 27:15)

26) P2: *"Have mercy upon us,"* (Psalm 6:3)

27) All: Come quickly to our help

28) P2: Show us why, despite all our zeal and achievements, we are still under your all-consuming wrath; show us why, despite all our knowledge and scholarship we have been repeatedly duped by false Messiahs who have brought us nothing but destruction, misery and ridicule. Show us also why our hopes in human progress have been repeatedly dashed. Are these failures signs that something is wrong with our religion? Have we got things so badly wrong both about you and human nature? Lord, please provide us with the strength to face reality and to accept your truth, Amen (Deuteronomy 4:24)

29) P1: Is it not time to consider the dreadful reality that in our religion there is a serious flaw preventing us from receiving divine blessing?

30) P2: It is indeed time to lay aside all our prejudices and consider this possibility, even though our minds are dismayed and our hearts sink within us. Our throats choke and our stomachs turnover, we waste away with anxiety, feelings of nausea overwhelm us. We are dizzy at the shock of how wrong we have been.

31) All: G-D PLEASE HAVE MERCY, REMEMBER YOUR COVENANTS AND PITY YOUR PEOPLE

32) P1: Let us take comfort from the knowledge that this time of destruction was predicted by the Holy Scriptures and has <u>not</u> come as a surprise to the Lord.

33) P2: For you, Lord, see everything and you are in control of all events. Nothing comes as a surprise to you. But *"how long, Oh Lord"* will it be before you deliver us? (Psalm 6:3b)

34) P1: Whilst acknowledging the fact that G-d knows everything in advance, let us now hear what the prophets say concerning our situation.

Begin <u>fourth</u> reading

1 Kings 8:26-62

26. *And now, oh G-d of Israel, let your word, I pray you, be verified, which you spoke unto your servant David my father.*

27. *But will G-d indeed dwell on the earth? Behold, the heaven and heaven of heavens cannot contain you; how much less this house that I have built?*

28. *Yet you have respected unto the prayer of your servant and to his supplication, Oh Lord" my G-d, to hearken unto the cry and to the prayer, which your servant prays before you today:*

29. *That your eyes may be open toward this house night and day, even toward the place of which you have said, my name shall be there: that*

you may hearken unto the prayer which your servant shall make toward this place.

30. And hearken you to the supplication of your servant and of your people Israel, when they shall pray toward this place: and hear you in heaven your dwelling place: and when you hear, forgive.

31. If any man trespass against his neighbour and an oath be laid upon him to cause him to swear and the oath come before your altar in this house:

32. Then hear you in heaven and do and judge your servants, condemning the wicked, to bring his way upon his head; and justifying the righteous, to give him according to his righteousness.

33. When your people Israel be smitten down before the enemy, because they have sinned against you and shall turn again to you and confess your name and pray and make supplication unto you in this house:

34. Then hear you in heaven and forgive the sin of your people Israel and bring them again unto the land, which you gave unto their fathers.

35. When heaven is shut up and there is no rain, because they have sinned against you; if they pray toward this place and confess your name and turn from their sin, when you afflict them:

36. Then hear you in heaven and forgive the sin of your servants and of your people Israel that you teach them the good way wherein they should walk and give rain upon your land, which you have given to your people for an inheritance.

37. If there be in the land famine, if there be pestilence, blasting, mildew, locust, or if there be caterpillar; if their enemy besiege them in the land of their cities; whatsoever plague, whatsoever sickness there be;

38. What prayer and supplication be made by any man, or by all your people Israel, which shall know every man the plague of his own heart and spread forth his hands toward this house:

39. Then hear you in heaven your dwelling place and forgive and do and give to every man according to his ways, whose heart you know; (for you, even you only, know the hearts of all the children of men;)

40. *That they may fear you all the days that they live in the land, which you gave unto our fathers.*

41. *Moreover, concerning a stranger that is not of your people Israel, but comes from a far country for your name's sake;*

42. *(For they shall hear of your great name and of your strong hand and of your stretched-out arm;) when he shall come and pray toward this house;*

43. *Hear you in heaven your dwelling place and do according to all that the stranger call to you for: that all people of the earth may know your name, to fear you, as do your people Israel; and that they may know that this house, which I have built, is called by your name.*

44. *If your people go out to battle against their enemy, whithersoever you shall send them and shall pray unto the Lord toward the city which you have chosen and toward the house that I have built for your name:*

45. *Then hear you in heaven their prayer and their supplication and maintain their cause.*

46. *If they sin against you, (for there is no man that sins not) and you be angry with them and deliver them to the enemy, so that they carry them away captives unto the land of the enemy, far or near;*

47. *Yet if they shall bethink themselves in the land whither they were carried captives and repent and make supplication unto you in the land of them that carried them captives, saying, 'We have sinned and have done perversely, we have committed wickedness;'*

48. *And so return unto you with all their heart and with all their soul, in the land of their enemies, which led them away captive and pray unto you toward their land, which you gave unto their fathers, the city, which you have chosen and the house which I have built for your name:*

49. *Then hear you their prayer and their supplication in heaven your dwelling place and maintain their cause*

50. *And forgive your people that have sinned against you and all their transgressions wherein they have transgressed against you and give them compassion before them who carried them captive, that they may have compassion on them:*

51. *For they are your people and your inheritance, which you brought forth out of Egypt, from the midst of the furnace of iron:*

52. *That your eyes may be open unto the supplication of your servant and unto the supplication of your people Israel, to hearken unto them in all that they call for unto you.*

53. *For you did separate them from among all the people of the earth, to be your inheritance, as you spoke by the hand of Moses your servant, when you brought our fathers out of Egypt, Oh Lord G-d.*

54. *And it was so, that when Solomon had made an end of praying all this prayer and supplication unto the Lord, he arose from before the altar of the Lord, from kneeling on his knees with his hands spread up to heaven.*

55. *And he stood and blessed all the congregation of Israel with a loud voice, saying,*

56. *Blessed be the Lord, that has given rest unto his people Israel, according to all that he promised: there has not failed one word of all his good promise, which he promised by the hand of Moses his servant.*

57. *The Lord our G-d is with us, as he was with our fathers: let him not leave us, nor forsake us:*

58. *That he may incline our hearts unto him, to walk in all his ways and to keep his commandments and his statutes and his judgments, which he commanded our fathers.*

59. *And let these my words, wherewith I have made supplication before the Lord, be nigh unto the Lord our G-d day and night, that he maintains the cause of his servant and the cause of his people Israel at all times, as the matter shall require:*

60. *That all the people of the earth may know that the Lord is G-d and that there is none else.*

61. *Let your heart therefore be perfect with the Lord our G-d, to walk in his statutes and to keep his commandments, as at this day.*

62. *And the king and all Israel with him, offered sacrifice before the Lord*

Isaiah 13:2f

2. Lift you up a banner upon the high mountain, exalt the voice unto them and wave the hand so that they may go into the gates of the nobles.

3. I have commanded my sanctified ones; I have also called my mighty ones for mine anger, even them that rejoice in my highness.

4. The noise of a multitude in the mountains, like as of a great people; a tumultuous noise of the kingdoms of nations gathered together: The Lord of hosts musters the host of the battle.

5. They come from a far country, from the end of heaven, even the Lord and the weapons of his indignation, to destroy the whole land.

6. Howl you; for the day of the Lord is at hand; it shall come as destruction from the Almighty.

7. Therefore shall all hands be faint and every man's heart shall melt:

8. And they shall be afraid: pangs and sorrows shall take hold of them; they shall be in pain as a woman that travails: they shall be amazed one at another; their faces shall be as flames.

9. Behold, the day of the Lord comes, cruel both with wrath and fierce anger, to lay the land desolate: and he shall destroy the sinners thereof out of it.

10. For the stars of heaven and the constellations thereof shall not give their light: the sun shall be darkened in his going forth and the moon shall not cause her light to shine.

11. And I will punish the world for their evil and the wicked for their iniquity; and I will cause the arrogance of the proud to cease and will lay low the haughtiness of the terrible.

12. I will make a man more precious than fine gold; even a man than the golden wedge of Ophir.

13. Therefore I will shake the heavens and the earth shall remove out of her place, in the wrath of the Lord of hosts and in the day of his fierce anger.

14. And it shall be as the chased roe and as a sheep that no man takes up: then shall every man turn to his own people and flee every one into his own land.

15. Every one that is found shall be thrust through; and every one that is joined unto them shall fall by the sword.

16. Their children also shall be dashed to pieces before their eyes; their houses shall be spoiled and their wives ravished.

17. Behold, I will stir up the Medes against them, who shall not regard silver; and as for gold, they shall not delight in it.

18. Their bows also shall dash the young men to pieces; and they shall have no pity on the fruit of the womb; their eyes shall not spare children.

19. And Babylon, the glory of kingdoms, the beauty of the Chaldean's pride, shall be as when G-d overthrew Sodom and Gomorrah.

20. It shall never be inhabited, neither shall it be dwelt in from generation to generation: neither shall the Arabians pitch tent there; neither shall the shepherds make their fold there.

21. But wild beasts of the desert shall lie there; and their houses shall be full of doleful creatures; and owls shall dwell there and satyrs shall dance there.

22. And the wild beasts of the islands shall cry in their desolate houses and dragons in their pleasant palaces: and her time is near to come and her days shall not be prolonged.

Zechariah 13:7f

7. Awake, oh sword, against my shepherd and against the man that is my fellow, says the Lord of hosts: smite the shepherd and the sheep shall be scattered: and I will turn mine hand upon the little ones.

8. And it shall come to pass, that in all the land, says the Lord two parts therein shall be cut off and die; but the third shall be left therein.

9. And I will bring the third part through the fire and will refine them as silver is refined and will try them as gold is tried: they shall call on my name and I will hear them: I will say, 'It is my people' and they shall say, 'The Lord is my G-d.'

Section 3: The 'Calling'

1) P1: *"Even though the sun shall be turned into darkness and the moon into blood before the great and terrible day of the Lord,"* (Joel 2:31) let us wholeheartedly and with a settled mind, trust that in His faithful mercy, G-d will honour His covenant promises to His people

2) P2: *"Whosoever shall call upon the name of the Lord <u>shall</u> be delivered,"* (Joel 2:32)

3) P1: This same promise applies to us today. As a group of sinners standing on the very brink of destruction, let us *"call upon the name of the Lord"*

Begin <u>fifth</u> reading,

The word *'Selah'* is an instruction meaning *'pause, reflect and think on that.'*

Psalm 81

1. Sing aloud unto G-d our strength: make a joyful noise unto the G-d of Jacob.

2. Take a psalm and bring hither the timbrel [drums], the pleasant harp with the psaltery.

3. Blow up the trumpet in the new moon, in the time appointed, on our solemn feast day.

4. For this was a statute for Israel and a law of the G-d of Jacob.

5. This he ordained in Joseph for a testimony, when he went out through the land of Egypt: where I heard a language that I understood not.

6. I removed his shoulder from the burden: his hands were delivered from the pots.

7. You called in trouble and I delivered you; I answered you in the secret place of thunder: I proved you at the waters of Meribah. Selah.

8. Hear, oh my people and I will testify unto you: oh Israel, if you will hearken unto me;

9. There shall no strange G-d be in you; neither shall you worship any strange G-d.

10. *I am the Lord your G-d, which brought you out of the land of Egypt: open your mouth wide and I will fill it.*

11. *But my people would not hearken to my voice; and Israel would have none of me.*

12. *So I gave them up unto their own hearts' lust: and they walked in their own counsels.*

13. *Oh, that my people had hearkened unto me and Israel had walked in my ways!*

14. *I should soon have subdued their enemies and turned my hand against their adversaries.*

15. *The haters of the Lord should have submitted themselves unto Him: but their time should have endured forever.*

16. *He [the Lord] should have fed them also with the finest of the wheat: and with honey out of the rock should I have satisfied you.*

Psalm 82

1. *G-d stands in the congregation of the mighty; he judges among the G-ds.*

2. *How long will you judge unjustly and accept the persons of the wicked? Selah.*

3. *Defend the poor and fatherless: do justice to the afflicted and needy.*

4. *Deliver the poor and needy: rid them out of the hand of the wicked.*

5. *They know not, neither will they understand; they walk on in darkness: all the foundations of the earth are out of course.*

6. *I have said, you are G-ds[8] and all of you are children of the highest.*

7. *But you shall die like men and fall like one of the princes.*

8. *Arise, oh G-d, judge the earth: for you shall inherit all nations.*

---

[8] The context of these words would suggest that deliberate irony is being employed here, aimed specifically at the godless who proudly think they are mini-gods, above and beyond any law

Psalm 83

1. Keep not you silence, oh G-d: hold not your peace and be not still, oh G-d.

2. For, lo, your enemies make a tumult: and they that hate you have lifted-up their head.

3. They have taken crafty counsel against your people and consulted against your hidden ones.

4. They have said, Come and let us cut them off from being a nation; that the name of Israel may be no more in remembrance.

5. For they have consulted together with one heart: they are confederate against you:

6. The tabernacles of Edom and the Ishmaelites; of Moab and the Hagarenes;

7. Gebal and Ammon and Amalek; the Philistines with the inhabitants of Tyre;

8. Assur also is joined with them: they have helped the children of Lot. Selah.

9. Do unto them as unto the Midianites; as to Sisera, as to Jabin, at the brook of Kishon:

10. Which perished at Endor: they became as dung for the earth.

11. Make their nobles like Oreb and like Zeeb: you, all their princes as Zebah and as Zalmunna:

12. Who said, 'Let us take to ourselves the houses of G-d in possession.'

13. Oh my G-d makes them like a whirling dust, as the stubble before the wind.

14. As the fire burns a wood and as the flame sets the mountains on fire;

15. *So persecute them with your tempest and make them afraid with your storm.*

16. *Fill their faces with shame; that they may seek your name, Oh Lord.*

17. *Let them be confounded and troubled forever; let them be put to shame and perish:*

18. *That men may know that you, whose name alone is JEHOVAH is the highest over all the earth.*

Psalm 84

1. *How amiable are your tabernacles, Oh Lord of hosts!*

2. *My soul longs, yea, even faints for the courts of the Lord: my heart and my flesh cry out for the living G-d.*

3. *The sparrow has found a house and the swallow a nest for herself, where she may lay her young, even your altars, Oh Lord of hosts, my King and my G-d.*

4. *Blessed are they that dwell in your house: they will be still praising you, Selah.*

5. *Blessed is the man whose strength is in you; in whose heart are your ways.*

6. *Who passing through the valley of Baca make it a well; the rain also fills the pools.*

7. *They go from strength to strength; every one of them in Zion appears before G-d.*

8. *Oh Lord G-d of hosts; hear my prayer: give ear, oh G-d of Jacob, Selah.*

9. *Behold, oh G-d our shield and look upon the face of your anointed.*

10. *For a day in your courts is better than a thousand. I had rather be a doorkeeper in the house of my G-d, than to dwell in the tents of wickedness.*

11. *For the Lord G-d is a sun and shield: The Lord will give grace and glory: no good thing will he withhold from them that walk uprightly.*

12. *Oh Lord of hosts, blessed is the man that trusts in you.*

Psalm 85

1. *Lord, you have been favourable unto your land: you have brought back the captivity of Jacob.*

2. *You have forgiven the iniquity of your people; you have covered all their sin. Selah.*

3. *You have taken away your entire wrath: you have turned yourself from the fierceness of your anger.*

4. *Turn to us, oh G-d of our salvation and cause your anger toward us to cease.*

5. *Will you* [continue to] *be angry with us forever? Will you draw out your anger to all generations?*

6. *Will you not revive us again: that your people may rejoice in you?*

7. *Show us your mercy, Oh Lord and grant us your salvation.*

8. *I will hear what G-d the Lord will speak: for he will speak peace unto his people and to his saints: but let them not turn again to folly.*

9. *Surely his salvation is nigh them that fear him; that glory may dwell in our land.*

10. *Mercy and truth are met together; righteousness and peace have kissed each other.*

11. *Truth shall spring out of the earth; and righteousness shall look down from heaven.*

12. *You, the Lord shall give that which is good; and our land shall yield her increase.*

13. *Righteousness shall go before him; and shall set us in the way of his steps*

4) P1: Lord, our situation is hopeless, (Isaiah 57:10)

5) P2: It is utterly hopeless, (Jeremiah 2:25 & 18:12)

6) P1: No human hand can save us

7) P2: Only you can save us, Oh Lord

8) P1: Our enemies are poised to destroy us

9) P2: They will show us no mercy; it is our destruction they want

10) P1: In contrast, you Lord delight in showing mercy to millions. As it is written *"The Lord is long-suffering and has great mercy, forgiving iniquity and transgression,"* (Numbers 14:18a).

11) All:
So, as one congregation we beg you during this time of Jacob's trouble, to: -
Save your heritage Oh Lord
Save your people Oh Lord
Save your nation Oh Lord
In this time of global destruction,
Save all who believe in your Holy Name –
For the sake of your one true Messiah,
Whoever he is,
Please answer this prayer

12) P1: We also ask you to *"Save [us] now! [We] beseech you Oh Lord! [We] beseech you, send"* deliverance, (Psalm 118:25)

13) All: *"Save [us] now! [We] beseech you Oh Lord! [We] beseech you, send"* deliverance, (Psalm 118:25)

14) P1:
Lord G-d of Abraham, Isaac and Jacob, (Exodus 3:6)
Lord G-d of Moses, Aaron and Joshua,
Lord G-d of Samuel, David and Solomon
Lord G-d of the prophets, priests and kings
Lord G-d of countless saints throughout the ages
Their G-d, our G-d,
We call upon you,
Yes! You the highest G-d of Israel,

15) All:
We call upon you, our Lord of Hosts to: -
> Outpour your Holy Spirit

and

Double, Treble
> And
>> Quadruple
>>> The number of Angels
>>>> Sent to guard us,

(Psalm 91:11)[9]

16) P1: In times past, G-d spoke to our fathers – prophesying the blessings and curses He would bring upon both Israel and the world, (Isaiah 24:4, 33:9 & Jeremiah 4:28) Seeing that these curses have already come to pass, let us cling to the certainty that the promises of blessing will also come to pass. In response, let us take comfort from the following words of Scripture: -

Begin <u>sixth</u> reading

Zechariah 12:1f

1. The burden of the word of the Lord for Israel, says the Lord, which stretches forth the heavens and lays the foundation of the earth and forms the spirit of man within him.

2. Behold, I will make Jerusalem a cup of trembling unto all the people round about, when they shall be in the siege both against Judah and against Jerusalem.

3. And in that day, will I make Jerusalem a burdensome stone for all the peoples: whoever lifts it shall be cut in pieces and all the nations on earth are gathered together against it.

4. In that day, says the Lord, I will smite every horse with astonishment and his rider with madness: and I will open mine eyes upon the house of Judah and will smite every horse of the people with blindness.

5. And the governors of Judah shall say in their heart, 'the inhabitants of Jerusalem shall have strength in the Lord of hosts their G-d.'

---

[9] The writer made this prayer in great desperation when physically attacked by an evil spirit on Holy Island on the evening of Monday, 6th September 1976. It's of special, personal value to him. The *'double, treble and quadruple'* phrase was suggested by Yevtushenko's poem *'The Heirs of Stalin,'* quoted before the contents page of Ginzburg (1968).

6. In that day will I make the governors of Judah like a hearth of fire among the wood and like a torch of fire in a sheaf; and they shall devour all the people round about, on the right hand and on the left: and Jerusalem shall be inhabited again in her own place, even in Jerusalem.

7. The Lord also shall save the tents of Judah first, that the glory of the house of David and the glory of the inhabitants of Jerusalem do not magnify themselves against Judah.

8. In that day shall the Lord defend the inhabitants of Jerusalem; and he that is feeble among them at that day shall be as David; and the house of David shall be as G-d, as the angel of the Lord before them.

9. And it shall come to pass in that day that I will seek to destroy all the nations that come against Jerusalem.

10. And I will pour upon the house of David and upon the inhabitants of Jerusalem, the spirit of grace and of supplications: and they shall look upon me whom they have pierced and they shall mourn for him, as one mourns for his only son and shall be in bitterness for him, as one that is in bitterness for his firstborn.

11. In that day there shall be great mourning in Jerusalem, as the mourning of Hadadrimmon in the valley of Megiddon.

12. And the land shall mourn, every family apart; the family of the house of David apart and their wives apart; the family of the house of Nathan apart and their wives apart;

13. The family of the house of Levi apart and their wives apart; the family of Shimei apart and their wives apart;

14. All the families that remain, every family apart and their wives apart.

Zechariah 13:1-2

1. In that day there shall be a fountain opened to the house of David and to the inhabitants of Jerusalem for sin and for uncleanness.

2. And it shall come to pass in that day, says the Lord of hosts, that I will cut off the names of the idols out of the land and they shall no more be remembered: and, I will cause the prophets and the unclean spirit to pass out of the land.

Malachi 4:1f

1. *For, behold, the day comes that shall burn as an oven; and all the proud, you and all that do wickedly, shall be stubble: and the day that comes shall burn them up, says the Lord of hosts, that it shall leave them neither root nor branch.*

2. *But to you who fear my name shall the sun of righteousness arise with healing in his wings; and you shall go forth and grow up as calves of the stall.*

3. *And you shall tread down the wicked; for they shall be ashes under the soles of your feet in the day that I shall do this, says the Lord of hosts.*

17) P1: These are promises which G-d <u>cannot</u> break, for He is always faithful to His word, (Deuteronomy 30:19 & Isaiah 45:23)

18) P2: All His promises are fulfilled to the smallest detail, Amen

19) All:
Dear, distant Lord,
<u>If</u> you are listening,
Remember the promises
Made in your Word

Please, turn
Defeat into victory,
Despair into hope,
Disbelief into faith,
Failure into success,
Hatred into love,
Illness into health,
Misery into joy,
Poverty into prosperity
And
Sin into holiness;

So, we may be ready
To do your will
Amidst
The biggest battle of our lives, Amen[10]

---

[10] Entitled *'Reversals'* this prayer was written on a coach during the evening of Saturday, 26th February 2005 and highlights the need to trust the Lord to reverse impossible situations

B: THE *'COMING TO FAITH'* SECTIONS

Section 4: The Invocation

1) P1: Bearing the promises of divine revelation in mind, let us now request our merciful Lord to send His Spirit of holiness to remove all sinful uncleanness and to heal any spiritual blindness which may be veiling our hearts

Pause

2) All:

Father of lights, Creator of all that is,
You who are faithful to your everlasting covenant;
We beseech you to send your Spirit of holiness
To expose the sin in our lives
And in the life of the Nation;
In Your great mercy
Please show us exactly where we have erred -
What cherished prejudices we need to forsake
And what unrighteous hatreds we must abandon

Pause

3) P1: Lord, help us in our unbelief

4) P2: Yes, help us in our unbelief

5) P1: Father, send Your Spirit of holiness (Psalms 89:26 & 103:13)

6) All: May He remove any veil preventing us from seeing your truth and from rightly interpreting your revelation.

7) P1: Father, send Your Holy Spirit

8) All: Please reveal the true Messiah and empower us to be your witnesses to all nations

9) P1: Father, let Your Holy Spirit be a fountain

10) All: Freely outpoured to cleanse us from all sin

11) P1: Whilst waiting for the Lord G-d of Israel to pour out His Spirit, let us draw comfort from the following promises of Scripture: -

Begin seventh reading

Jeremiah 3:12-18

12. *Go and proclaim these words toward the north and say, 'Return, backsliding Israel,' 'says the Lord; 'and I will not cause mine anger to fall upon you: for I am merciful,' says the Lord and I will not keep anger forever'.*

13. *Only acknowledge your iniquity, that you have transgressed against the Lord your G-d and have scattered your ways to the strangers under every green tree and you have not obeyed my voice, says the Lord.*

14. *Turn, oh backsliding children, says the Lord; for I am married unto you: and I will take you one of a city and two of a family and I will bring you to Zion:*

15. *And I will give you pastors according to mine heart, which shall feed you with knowledge and understanding.*

16. *And it shall come to pass, when you be multiplied and increased in the land, in those days, says the Lord, they shall say no more, The Ark of the Covenant of the Lord: neither shall it come to mind: neither shall they remember it; neither shall they visit it; neither shall that be done any more.*

17. *At that time they shall call Jerusalem the throne of the Lord; and all the nations shall be gathered unto it, to the name of the Lord, to Jerusalem: neither shall they walk any more after the imagination of their evil heart.*

18. *In those days the house of Judah shall walk with the house of Israel and they shall come together out of the land of the north to the land that I have given for an inheritance unto your fathers.*

Ezekiel 36:25f

25. *Then will I sprinkle clean water upon you and you shall be clean: from all your filthiness and from all your idols, will I cleanse you.*

26. *A new heart also will I give you and a new spirit will I put within you: and I will take away the stony heart out of your flesh and I will give you a heart of flesh.*

27. And I will put my spirit within you and cause you to walk in my statutes and you shall keep my judgments and do them.

28. And you shall dwell in the land that I gave to your fathers; and you shall be my people and I will be your G-d.

29. I will also save you from all your uncleanness: and I will call for the corn and will increase it and lay no famine upon you.

30. And I will multiply the fruit of the tree and the increase of the field, that you shall receive no more reproach of famine among the heathen.

31. Then shall you remember your own evil ways and your doings that were not good and shall loath yourselves in your own sight for your iniquities and for your abominations.

32. Not for your sakes do I this, says the Lord G-d, be it known unto you: be ashamed and confounded for your own ways, Oh house of Israel.

33. Thus says the Lord G-d; in the day that I shall have cleansed you from all your iniquities I will also cause you to dwell in the cities and the wastes shall be built.

34. And the desolate land shall be tilled, whereas it lay desolate in the sight of all that passed by.

35. And they shall say, this land that was desolate is become like the Garden of Eden; and the wastes and desolate and ruined cities are become fenced and are inhabited.

36. Then the heathen that are left round about you shall know that I the Lord build the ruined places and plant that that was desolate: I the Lord have spoken it and I will do it.

37. Thus says the Lord G-d; I will yet for this be enquired of by the house of Israel, to do it for them; I will increase them with men like a flock.

38. As the holy flock, as the flock of Jerusalem in her solemn feasts; so, shall the waste cities be filled with flocks of men: and they shall know that I am the Lord!

Joel 2:27f.

27. *And you shall know that I am amid Israel and that I am the Lord your G-d and none else: and my people shall never be ashamed.*

28. *And it shall come to pass afterward, that I will pour out my spirit upon all mankind; and your sons and your daughters shall prophesy, your old men shall dream dreams, your young men shall see visions:*

29. *And upon the servants and upon the handmaids in those days will I pour out my spirit.*

30. *And I will show wonders in the heavens and in the earth, blood and fire and pillars of smoke.*

31. *The sun shall be turned into darkness and the moon into blood, before the great and terrible day of the Lord come.*

32. *And it shall come to pass, that whosoever shall call on the name of the Lord shall be delivered: for in mount Zion and in Jerusalem shall be deliverance, as the Lord has said and in the remnant whom the Lord shall call.*

Pause

12) P1: Dear Father of Israel

13) P2:
We are desperate
We are hopeless
We are on the eve of destruction
The entire world[11]
Is arrayed against us,
No one stands by your people
We are no longer included among the nations, (Numbers 23:9)
Our isolation is complete
Please prevent us from
Going into exile again

---

[11] Suggested here is something more extreme than another united Arab (or Arab-Iranian) assault upon Israel. Bible prophecy seems to imply at least two assaults; the first (possibly a united Arab or Arab-Iranian one) would force the Jewish people to accept the anti-Christ to gain some peace, (John 5:43b). The second assault would come about because of a *'falling out'* with the anti-Christ directly related to his demands to be worshipped as G-d (Matthew 24:15). It is this second global assault which will oblige them to reconsider the claims of the true Messiah. Each scenario would suggest that there will be at least two major attempts to destroy the Jewish people before Christ's return.

See what our enemies have done to us!
They have deceived us,
They have slain our families and friends,
They press in ruthlessly to destroy us
Employing the latest weapons of mass destruction
To accomplish their evil aims
Many are the charred corpses in Israel.
The wounded sicken and die
For we have nothing to sustain them
Hunger tightens our stomachs and
Thirst parches our tongues
Our supplies are at an end,
Our strength is no more
Our helplessness is complete

For the sake of your great and holy name,
Remember your covenant promises
Made to Abraham and our forefathers
Show your justice to those who would destroy us
Strike them down with
The plagues of Egypt, (Exodus 7-12)
Judge them with fire, (2 Kings 1:9-12)
And blot them from the face of the earth, (Psalm 69:28)

Please do not ignore the many sufferings they have inflicted upon us,
"The apple of" your eye (Zechariah 2:8c)[12]

For psychological and emotional relief words from the imprecatory Psalms (e.g. Psalm 137) may be read aloud. These should give an opportunity for people to release any feelings of hatred they may have.

14) P1: Yet remember that vengeance belongs to G-d and not to us, (Deuteronomy 32:35 & Psalm 94:1)

15) P2: Into Your hands, Oh Lord we commend all our enemies for you to either judge or to give the gift of forgiveness, following their genuine repentance, Amen

16) P1: As one people let us plead for the Lord to remove the evil that dwells in our own hearts. Surely, if it were not for His tender mercy, we too, in character, would be like our enemies.

---

[12] These words (from *'for the sake of...'*) may not be acceptable from a Christian viewpoint but they will be necessary for emotional release

17) All:
We acknowledge that
All our traditions and good works
Have availed us nothing

Our own Rabbis have misled us,
When they have suggested
We could merit your favour
By trying to follow your Law

We failed to see that
The standards in your Law
Were too high for any person
To obey with the complete perfection
That your holiness requires.
Our view of human nature has been unrealistic –
Woefully underestimating the extent to which sin
Dominates the human heart

We also grievously polluted ourselves
With many wretched
Superstitious and magical practices,
Condemned in your Word

Many of us have slavishly followed
A counterfeit mysticism
Fabricated by Satan
To blind us to the true Messiah
And loose us in vain philosophical speculation[13]

As a people, we have been disobedient
In trying to find our own way to please you;
Pride has lain at the root of our religion

Please forgive us!
Send Your Spirit of holiness to redeem us
And to bring us into a right relationship with you
Guard us with your mighty angels

Hear our groans
Just as you did when we were slaves in Egypt, (Exodus 2:24f & 3:7-9)
Break the stranglehold of sin in our lives
Show us the true Messiah
And restore your blessings to Israel

---

[13] Reference is made here to the practices associated with Jewish Cabbalistic mysticism.

Be faithful to your Covenant
And fulfil the promises of your Word
In Your great mercy
Please hear our prayer
Come <u>now</u> and save us, Amen

Section 5: The Recognition

As the veil of unbelief is removed a numbed silence may follow. This, in turn, may give way to convulsive weeping or prostration before the Lord. There may be a recapitulation of Paul's experience upon the Damascus Road, or of King Josiah's upon hearing the reading of the Law in 2 Kings 22:11 & 2 Chronicles 34:19. In some cases the following dialogue may take place.[14]

1) Q: *"Who are you Lord?"* (Acts 9:5a)

2) M: *"I am Yeshua whom you persecute: it is hard to kick against the pricks"*[15] (Acts 9:5b)

3) Q: *"What are these wounds in your hands?"* (Zechariah 13:6a)

4) M: *"These I received in the house of my friends"* (Zechariah 13:6b)

Pause to allow time for the shock of these words to be absorbed. Further convulsive weeping may well take place

5) M: *"Now, do not be grieved or angry with yourselves that you sold me beforehand. For G-d sent me before you to preserve life, to preserve your posterity* [you and your descendants] *in the earth and to save your lives by a great deliverance,"* (Genesis 45:7 & 9)

Begin eighth reading

Isaiah 52:13-53:1f

13. *Behold, my servant shall deal prudently, he shall be exalted and extolled and be very high.*

14. *As many were astonished* [because] *his visage was so marred more than any man and his form more than the sons of men:*

15. *So shall he sprinkle many nations; the kings shall shut their mouths at him: for that which had not been told them shall they see; and that which they had not heard shall they consider.*

1. *Who has believed our report? And to whom is the arm of the Lord revealed?*

---

[14] The writer was much stirred in his heart when he finally word-processed this short dialogue (on Monday, 27th July 1998). He felt as if he were launching upon something holy and profound. This feeling also manifested itself on Thursday, 29th November 2007 when correcting another draft and again whilst praying at The Wailing Wall in Jerusalem on Passover Friday, 14th April 2017.

[15] *'Pricks'* or *'goads'* were long, pointed sticks used as a *'cattle prod'* to guide livestock in a certain direction.

2. *For he shall grow up before him as a tender plant and as a root out of a dry ground: he has neither form nor comeliness; and when we shall see him there is no beauty that we should desire him.*

3. *He is despised and rejected of men; a man of sorrows and acquainted with grief: and we hid as it were our faces from him; he was despised and we esteemed him not.*

4. *Surely, he has borne our grief and carried our sorrows: yet we did esteem him stricken, smitten of G-d and afflicted.*

5. *But he was wounded for our transgressions; he was bruised for our iniquities: the chastisement of our peace was upon him; and with his stripes we are healed.*

6. *All we like sheep have gone astray; we have turned everyone to his own way; and the Lord has laid on him the iniquity of us all.*

7. *He was oppressed and he was afflicted, yet he opened not his mouth: he is brought as a lamb to the slaughter and as a sheep before her shearers is dumb, so he opened not his mouth.*

8. *He was taken from prison and from judgment: and who shall declare his generation? For he was cut off out of the land of the living: for the transgression of my people was he stricken.*

9. *And he made his grave with the wicked and with the rich in his death; because he had done no violence, neither was any deceit in his mouth.*

10. *Yet it pleased the Lord to bruise him; he has put him to grief: when you shall make his soul an offering for sin, he shall see his seed, he shall prolong his days and the pleasure of the Lord shall prosper in his hand.*

11. *He shall see of the travail of his soul and shall be satisfied: by his knowledge shall my righteous servant justify many; for he shall bear their iniquities.*

13. *Therefore will I divide him a portion with the great and he shall divide the spoil with the strong; because he has poured out his soul unto death: and he was numbered with the transgressors; and he bears the sin of many and makes intercession for the transgressors.*

Section 6: How Could We?

1) All:

1.
How could we have been so foolish?[16]
How could we have been so deaf?
How could we have been so blind?

2.
We had gazed upon the Messiah
Yet we never recognised Him.
We had benefited from the Lord's blessings
Yet we failed to perceive it when they were taken away

3.
We had been stewards of divine revelation -
Yet we ourselves could not live up to its teaching.
Yes! As Moses said;
We *"are a stubborn and stiff-necked people,"* (Deuteronomy 9:6b)
Our sins had almost consumed us,
But in Your mercy a remnant has been preserved (Isaiah 1:9)
To bring honour to your great Name

4.
We suffer from great and mounting distress
Our hearts break within us,
Our minds are numbed with shock,
Our bodies tremble in dismay.
We stagger and sway
Under the weight of our sins
For now, we see <u>you,</u> Yeshua,
The son of David, our Messiah
Whose pierced hands
Are outstretched in greeting, (Zechariah 12:10)

5.
Now,
All delusion has gone,
All rebellion cast aside,
All proud self-justification completely discarded;
Every worthless idol has been repudiated,

---

[16] First drafted on Friday 25th April 1986, this meditation vividly conveys the psychological shock many Jews may feel upon discovering who the Messiah really is. It is assumed however, that such a realisation will only take place during a time of great suffering for the Jewish people, possibly in the context of a global holocaust and a massive environmental disaster – which the writer sincerely hopes he will not live to see.

The mighty hand of G-d has humbled us,
He has shattered our pride
And caused us to lose faith in ourselves

6.
What can we do?
The unthinkable has happened
The impossible has taken place
The unspeakable is now a fact.
We Jews have become believers in Yeshua!
Yet we remain as Jews and
Indeed, in some ways we are
More Jewish than before!

7.
Our sins were terrible
Hateful in Your sight;
Yet in your amazing grace,
You forgave them
Because of the blood sacrifice of your Messiah!
Our self-righteousness has gone –
Dispersed like the morning mist.
Our pride has dried up and withered away
As if it were a desert flower

8.
Lord, forgive us for not receiving you
Please do not condemn us for our sins
Pour out Your wonderful mercies
Immerse us in your forgiveness
Take heed of our tears of repentance.
For the sake of our ancestors
Please do not disregard us
Your children in this hour of trial
Yeshua, Our Messiah,
Have mercy upon us sinners,
And honour your promises,
Made to Abraham, Isaac and Jacob, Amen

2) P1: Come let us trust that the Lord has forgiven us [17]

3) P2: We will celebrate and praise the true Messiah

4) P1: Let us do this now!

---

[17] The prayers from *'Come let us...'* were first drafted on Saturday 1st December 2007

5) All:
Hosanna to the Son of David!

Blessed is He who comes in the name of the Lord (Psalm 118:26a)

Hosanna in the Highest!

Blessed is He who comes in the name of the Lord, even the King of Israel, (Matthew 21:9; 23:39 & John 12:13)

Blessed is He who comes in the name of the Lord (Luke 13:35 & 19:38)

Hosanna in the highest!
Hosanna in the highest!
Hosanna in the highest!
Hosanna in the highest!

C: PRAISE AND PLEADING SECTIONS

Section 7: Messianic Praise

1) P1: *"It is <u>my</u> people!"* (Zechariah 13:9c)[18]

2) All: *"The Lord is <u>my</u> G-d,"* (Zechariah 13:9d)

3) P1: You, *"Rabbi"* Yeshua *"are <u>the</u> Son of G-d, <u>the</u> King of Israel,"* (John 1:49b)

4) All: You are *"<u>my</u> Lord and <u>my</u> G-d,"* (John 20:28)

5) P1: You are *"the Messiah, the <u>Son</u> of the living G-d,"* (Daniel 3:25c & Matthew 16:16b)

6) All: Who has refined us in the fires of great tribulation, (Acts 14:22b)

7) P1: It is the Spirit of G-d who has shown us these truths. Our own natural minds could <u>never</u> have perceived them, (1 Corinthians 2:14)

8) All: *"Not by might, nor by power, but by my Spirit, says the Lord of Hosts,"* (Zechariah 4:6)

9) P1: You, Yeshua are worthy of all adoration and praise

10) All: *"Blessed is He that comes in the name of the Lord"* (Psalm 118:26a)

Pause: A time of spontaneous adoration may follow.

---

[18] The writer would proffer the very real possibility that the Lord Himself may speak some of the words (those spoken by the Presiding Participant) in this section. (This will be because He is revealing His very existence to the surviving remnant of Israel, just as He did to Paul on the Damascus Road – see **Appendix 1**).

Section 8: Pleading for the Messiah's Return

1) P1: Having recognised the Messiah who is the true Saviour of both Israel and of all those redeemed from every nation; let us now plead for His return from Heaven. Let us also pray for the firm establishment of His kingdom upon Earth, realising that *"Unless these days* [of great tribulation] *be shortened no flesh will be saved,"* (Matthew 24:22a) and all human life would be extinguished.

2) P2: *"But for the elect's sake those days will be shortened"* (Matthew 24:22b)

3) P1: As one people under G-d and His Messiah-Yeshua; let us now use a prayer of Moses...

4) All: *"Rise up, Lord and let your enemies be scattered; Let them that hate you flee before you. Return Oh Lord to the many thousands of Israel,"* (Numbers 10:35b & 36b)

Begin ninth reading

Psalm 79

1. *Oh G-d, the heathens are come into your inheritance; your holy temple have they defiled; they have laid Jerusalem in heaps.*

2. *The dead bodies of your servants have they given to be meat unto the fowls of the heaven, the flesh of your saints unto the beasts of the earth.*

3. *Their blood have they shed like water round about Jerusalem; and there was none to bury them.*

4. *We are become a reproach to our neighbours, a scorn and derision to them that are round about us.*

5. *How long, Lord? Will you be angry forever? Shall your jealousy burn like fire?*

6. *Pour out your wrath upon the heathen that have not known you and upon the kingdoms that have not called upon your name.*

7. *For they have devoured Jacob and lay waste his dwelling place.*

8. *Oh remember not against us former iniquities: let your tender mercies speedily protect us: for we are brought very low.*

9. *Help us, oh G-d of our salvation, for the glory of your name: and deliver us and purge away our sins, for your name's sake.*

10. *Wherefore should the heathen say, 'where is their G-d?' Let him be known among the heathen in our sight by the revenging of the blood of your servants, which is shed.*

11. *Let the sighing of the prisoner come before you; according to the greatness of your power preserve those that are appointed to die;*

12. *And render unto our neighbours sevenfold into their bosom their reproach, wherewith they have reproached you, Oh Lord.*

13. *So we your people and the sheep of your pasture will give you thanks forever: we will show forth your praise to all generations.*

Psalm 80

1. *Give ear, oh Shepherd of Israel, you that lead Joseph like a flock; you that dwell between the cherubim's shine forth.*

2. *Before Ephraim and Benjamin and Manasseh stir up your strength and come and save us.*

3. *Turn us again, oh G-d and cause your face to shine; and we shall be saved.*

4. *Oh Lord G-d of hosts, how long will you be angry against the prayer of your people?*

5. *You fed them with the bread of tears; and gave them tears to drink in great measure.*

6. *You made us strife for our neighbours: and our enemies laughed among themselves.*

7. *Turn us again, oh G-d of hosts and cause your face to shine; and we shall be saved.*

8. *You have brought a vine out of Egypt: you have cast out the heathen and planted it.*

9. *You prepared room before it and did cause it to take deep root and it filled the land.*

10. *The hills were covered with the shadow of it and the boughs thereof were like the goodly cedars.*

11. *She sent out her boughs unto the sea and her branches unto the river.*

12. *Why have you then broken down her hedges, so that all they who pass by the way do pluck her?*

13. *The boar out of the wood does waste it and the wild beast of the field doth devour it.*

14. *Return, we beseech you, oh G-d of hosts: look down from heaven and behold and visit this vine;*

15. *And the vineyard, which your right hand has planted and the branch that you made strong for yourself.*

16. *It is burned with fire, it is cut down: they perish at the rebuke of your countenance.*

17. *Let your hand be upon the man of your right hand, upon the son of man whom you made strong for yourself.*

18. *So will not we go back from you: quicken us and we will call upon your name*

19. *Turn us again, Oh Lord G-d of hosts, cause your face to shine; and we shall be saved*

Isaiah 63:17-19

17. *Oh Lord, why have you made us to err from your ways and hardened our heart from your fear? Return for your servants' sake, the tribes of your inheritance.*

18. *The people of your holiness have possessed it but a little while: our adversaries have trodden down your sanctuary.*

19. *We are yours: you never barest rule over them; they were not called by your name.*

Isaiah 64:1-4

1. *Oh that you would rend the heavens, that you would come down, that the mountains might flow down at your presence,*

2. *As when the melting fire burns, the fire causes the waters to boil, to make your name known to your adversaries that the nations may tremble at your presence!*

3. *When you did terrible things, which we looked not for, you came down; the mountains flowed down at your presence.*

4. *For since the beginning of the world men have not heard, nor perceived by the ear, neither has the eye seen, oh G-d, beside you, what he has prepared for him that waits for him.*

A time of spontaneous prayer may follow the readings.

5) P1: *"Even so, come Lord Yeshua,"* (Revelation 22:19)

6) P2: Come quickly and save us in this our hour of peril.

7) P1: Save too the world you have created, let it not be given over to chaos and do <u>not</u> allow it to be destroyed by fire as it was destroyed by flood in the days of Noah, (Genesis 7:4-8:4)

8) P2: Remember your promise to save those who call upon you, (Joel 2:32)

9) P1: Keep your word and accept our thanks and praise

10) P2: Honour your promises and we will rejoice

11) All: Save us and we will testify to your goodness – so all the nations upon the earth will know that you are great and full of compassion!

Section 9: Rejoice, Oh Israel!

1) P1: Let us look up from our situation to the Lord, our Provider[19]

2) All:
The Lord is our King and our Saviour

He has opened a fountain of forgiveness
To the House of David
He has cleansed Jerusalem from all its sin

He will grant us victory
He will grant us triumph
He will grant us deliverance
And remove the harm caused by
Centuries of hate-filled prejudice

3) P1:
Rejoice! Rejoice! Oh Israel!
Because of the forgiveness granted to you
Shout out the Gospel from the rooftops!
Send it forth over the media networks!
Publicise it abroad to all the nations
For the sake of His Holy Name!
Rejoice! Rejoice! Oh Israel!
For the Lord has done an astonishing work
His enemies are dumbfounded
The media commentators are dismayed
Unbelievers across the world are aghast
At what the Lord has done

Rejoice! Rejoice! Oh Israel!

Premature obituaries written concerning you
Are being consigned to *'editorial wastepaper bins'*
Those commentators who *'wrote you off'*
Are being made to look foolish
Renowned *'Middle Eastern experts'*
Mumble confused apologies
The predictions of men have been confounded
And the entire World is astir
With news of your revelation

---

[19] Vividly portrayed is the joy that will be felt when the Jewish remnant discovers that their relationship with G-d has been restored. This dialogue was written on Friday 25th April 1986, following *'How could we?*

Rejoice! Rejoice! Oh Israel
Rejoice with thanksgiving
Shout aloud your testimony!
Be bold in your witness!
Call upon the Lord for further strength
And speak to the nations concerning His Messiah

4) All:
Lord we rejoice greatly in your salvation
The work of Your Spirit has enthralled us
We are exhilarated by your sense of glory

Like a fruitful vine
Our witness will spread
To the ends of the earth
We will tell all peoples everywhere
Of the Messiah's goodness to us

Arise and by your great strength
Deal with those enemies
Who long to destroy us!
Continue to display your victorious power and might
So that all nations will acknowledge you
As we do now

5) P1: *"Even so, come Lord Yeshua"* in all your Messianic glory (Revelation 22:19)

6) P2: Come quickly to defeat the powers of evil that rage against us

7) All: For we are your chosen people, Israel, *"the apple of* [your] *eye"*

Begin <u>tenth</u> reading

Zechariah 14:1-4

1. *Behold, the day of the Lord comes and your spoil shall be divided amid you.*

2. *For I will gather all nations against Jerusalem to battle; and the city shall be taken and the houses rifled and the women ravished; and half of the city shall go forth into captivity and the residue of the people shall not be cut off from the city.*

3. *Then shall the Lord go forth and fight against those nations, as when he fought in the day of battle.*

4. *And his feet shall stand in that day upon the Mount of Olives, which is before Jerusalem on the east and the Mount of Olives shall cleave in the midst thereof toward the east and toward the west and there shall be a very great valley; and half of the mountain shall remove toward the north and half of it toward the south.*

Revelation 19:11f

11. *And I saw heaven opened and behold a white horse; and he that sat upon him was called 'Faithful and True' and in righteousness he does judge and make war.*

12. *His eyes were as a flame of fire and on his head, were many crowns; and he had a name written, that no man knew, but himself.*

13. *And he was clothed with a vesture* [royal robe] *dipped in blood: and his name is called 'The Word of G-d.'*

14. *And the armies, which were in Heaven, followed him upon white horses, clothed in fine linen, white and clean.*

15. *And out of his mouth goes a sharp sword, that with it he should smite the nations: and he shall rule them with a rod of iron: and he treads the winepress of the fierceness and wrath of Almighty G-d.*

16. *And he has on his vesture and on his thigh a name written,* **KING OF KINGS and LORD OF LORDS.**

17. *And I saw an angel standing in the sun; and he cried with a loud voice, saying to all the fowls that fly amid heaven, 'Come and gather together unto the supper of the great G-d;'*

18. *That you may eat the flesh of kings and the flesh of captains and the flesh of mighty men and the flesh of horses and of them that sit on them and the flesh of all men, both free and bond, both small and great.'*

19. *And I saw the beast and the kings of the earth and their armies, gathered together to make war against him that sat on the horse and against his army.*

20. *And the beast was taken and with him the false prophet that wrought miracles before him, with which he deceived them that had received the mark of the beast and them that worshipped his image. These both were cast alive into a lake of fire burning with brimstone.*

21. *And the remnant was slain with the sword of him that sat upon the horse, which sword proceeded out of his mouth: and all the fowls were filled with their flesh.*

Revelation 20:1-6

1. *And I saw an angel come down from heaven, having the key of the bottomless pit and a great chain in his hand.*

2. *And he laid hold on the dragon, that old serpent, which is the Devil and Satan and bound him a thousand years,*

3. *And cast him into the bottomless pit and shut him up and set a seal upon him, that he should deceive the nations no more, till the thousand years should be fulfilled: and after that he must be loosed a little season.*

4. *And I saw thrones and they sat upon them and judgment was given unto them: and I saw the souls of them that were beheaded for the witness of Jesus and for the word of G-d and which had not worshipped the beast, neither his image, neither had received his mark upon their foreheads, or in their hands; and they lived and reigned with Christ a thousand years.*

5. *But the rest of the dead lived not again until the thousand years were finished. This is the first resurrection.*

6. *Blessed and holy is he that has part in the first resurrection: on such the second death has no power, but they shall be priests of G-d and of Christ and shall reign with him a thousand years.*

8) P1: Let us [recall and] celebrate the mighty victory He [just] gained for us

The Presiding Participant reads the verse whilst all join in to say the chorus *'Alleluia!'*

1. The Lord has vindicated His Word,

Alleluia!

2. He keeps all His promises,

Alleluia!

3. Our enemies have been confounded,

Alleluia!

4. They pressed in hard but were defeated,

Alleluia!

5. We were rescued when destruction faced us,

Alleluia!

6. Victory belongs to our G-d,

Alleluia!

7. He honours those who are faithful,

Alleluia!

8. He comforts His hard-pressed servants,

Alleluia!

9. Amidst many trials, He comforts them,

Alleluia!

10. May His name be glorified forever,

Alleluia!

11. The Lord has vindicated His Word,

Alleluia!

12. This brings immense joy and relief to our hearts,

Alleluia![20]

9) P1: Be grateful and go! Follow the Lord and His one true Messiah – serving Him in ways that will please Him and delight His Spirit of Holiness.

10) P2: This we gladly do, in appreciation of the wonderful mercies shown to us by our Heavenly Father through His Messiah, Alleluia!

---

[20] This meditation was written on Wednesday, 19th December 2007 – before being amended and inserted into this liturgy during Friday, 4th January 2008

D: CLOSING SECTION

60

Section 10: Fulfilment

1) M: *"The Lord bless you and keep you, the Lord make His face to shine upon you and be gracious to you, the Lord lift up His countenance upon you and give you peace,"* (Numbers 6:24-26)

In some cases, the Messiah Himself, at His discretion, may say the following words to faithful individuals;

2) M: *"Well done, you good and faithful servant. You have been faithful in a few things, I will make you ruler over many things. Enter into the joy of your Lord, Amen"* (Matthew 25:21 & 23)

On every anniversary of Israel's recognition of Jesus as the Messiah the following material may be added;

3) P1: In this time of world peace and blessing let us be thankful that our good Lord fulfils every one of His promises, down to their very last detail

4) P2: He is <u>always</u> *'faithful and true'* to His Word, Amen (Revelation 19:11b)

5) P1: He can never lie or mislead or lure us into any form of sin (James 1:13-15)

6) P2: Because He is righteous, holy and loving, Amen

7) P1:
Let us remember <u>these</u> things[21] <u>before</u> Satan is released from his confinement and allowed to deceive the nations once more. For, be warned, when this time of global blessing is over there will be another period of great trial in which this liturgy[22] will be said with the same desperation that characterised its first use. At this future time, *"Satan shall be loosed out of his prison and shall go out to deceive the nations which are in the four quarters of the earth, Gog and Magog, to gather them together to battle: the number of whom is as the sand of the sea. And they went up on the breadth of the earth and compassed the camp of the saints about and the beloved city: and fire came down from G-d out of heaven and devoured them. And the devil that deceived them was cast into the lake of fire and brimstone, where the beast and the false prophet are and shall be tormented day and night forever and ever,"* (Revelation 20:7-10).

---

[21] These *'things'* include the words just spoken and all of the contents of this liturgy.
[22] This does not exclude the possibility of there being minor modifications made to this liturgy, adapting its use other troublesome situations.

8) P2: These things will surely happen, just as Israel's recognition of the Messiah happened. G-d <u>always</u> fulfils His unconditional promises.

9) P1: And may those who live through this future time of deception keep faithful to the Word and remember how the Lord blessed and saved our forebears when they too stood on the brink of destruction, just before our Messiah's return.

10) P2: May this be so, Amen

11) P1: *"The grace of our Lord Yeshua, Messiah, be with you all, Amen"* (Revelation 22:21)

12) P2: May He quickly bring a new heaven and a new earth, where we can dwell with Him forever in perfect joy, Amen (Revelation 21:1-4)

13) P1: We shall live with Him forever

14) All: In a kingdom that has no end, Amen

After a brief pause, a final chorus, hymn or psalm of praise may be sung.

(Should the assembled group linger too long, the Presiding Participant should don his coat and move toward the exit door, further emphasising that the session has ended!)

APPENDICES

Appendix 1:
Saul of Tarsus: The Forerunner of Israel

(Zechariah 12:1-13.6; Acts 9:1-20, 22;1-21, 26:2-23 & Revelation 7:1f)

This Appendix originally consisted of hand-written notes for a sermon,[23] preached to twenty-five people at a now long closed Messianic Jewish fellowship on Friday, 25th October 1991. Their response had been positive although divisions within the leadership ensured that this assembly closed in January 1993. Only slight amendments to the wording were necessary when it was prepared for publication in August 2003. It enables readers to see how Saul's Damascus Road experience acted as a foreshadow of what G-d will do for the Jewish nation at a time of major global turmoil and apostasy within the Gentile Church. It acknowledges that it is always G-d who takes the initiative in our salvation; no human response is possible without an initial infusion of divine grace.

1) The three main characters in Acts 9:1-20 were: -
1.1 Saul – the proud but troubled Pharisee
1.2 Ananias – the knowledgeable but timid believer
1.3 Yeshua – who confronted Saul and Ananias by direct revelation

2) The two main stages of salvation were: -
2.1 An act of divine grace affecting all areas of Saul's personality
2.2 An act of human response – of repentance and faith in Yeshua

3) Saul's example indicates that the religious Orthodox, as well as the non-religious secular wings of Judaism needs a revelation of Yeshua as the Messiah

4) The intrinsic characteristics of Saul's experience on the Damascus Road were: -
4.1 His preparation beforehand through the preaching of Stephen (Acts 7:54 & 8:1)
4.2 Finding himself in a desperate situation where his pride had been humbled
4.3 Its sudden and unexpected nature
4.4 The overwhelming intensity of the experience (which was enough to change the direction of his life)
4.5 The ability of the experience to prepare Saul for his future ministry and the sufferings associated with it
4.6 The necessity of a very thorough pastoral follow-up from a mature believer – Ananias
4.7 Christ's personal revelation to Saul and his response to this, acting as a foretaste of Israel's recognition of the Messiah

---

[23] This was one of those sermons which flowed from the pen as it was being prepared.

5) The most probable characteristics constituting Israel's future national recognition of Yeshua as the Messiah would be: -
5.1 Prior psychological preparation for this event through various forms of faithful Christian witness
5.2 Prior gospel witness given by Jewish evangelists[24]
5.3 The event taking place when Israel is on the brink of annihilation
5.4 It being sudden enough to astonish both the Church and the World
5.5 That this event would powerfully affect all parts of Israeli society
5.6 It leading to a worldwide revival of faith in Yeshua as the Messiah and the salvation of many people from all national groups
5.7 The presence of an Ananias-type ministry to assist those Jewish people who've recognised Yeshua as their Messiah

6) G-d had a reasonable discussion with Ananias – showing that He can speak plainly to both the heart and the mind. Therefore, the example of Ananias clearly refutes the false teaching that *"G-d speaks only to the heart."* Such teaching is inadequate because it: -
6.1 Fails to make use of all available biblical data (Isaiah 1:18-20 & Acts 17:10-12)
6.2 Seeks to by-pass the human mind (with its capacity to use logic and reason)
6.3 Places unnecessary restrictions upon divine sovereignty
6.4 Stems from eastern religious thought-forms, especially associated with both Hinduism and Buddhism
6.5 Makes nonsense of Jewish customs *e.g.* the wrapping of the Tefkin around the forehead, signifying the word *'speaking'* to the mind
6.6 Can lead to deception and personal manipulation because the mind is not allowed to *"test all things"* (1 Thessalonians 5:21 & 1 John 4:1)
6.7 Encourages an undiscerning acceptance of any teaching (whether true or false, good or bad) by fostering an attitude, which states *"if it feels good, it's right to receive it"*

7) An *'Ananias'* type ministry is one characterised by: -
7.1 A definite personal calling to exercise such a ministry
7.2 A willingness to help new Jewish believers
7.3 Sharing the love of Yeshua in whatever manner is appropriate
7.4 Witnessing and defending the claims of Yeshua as the Messiah
7.5 A *'building up'* of Jewish believers who are young in the faith
7.6 The responsible use of spiritual gifts in a flexible manner

---

[24] They themselves would have come to recognise the Messiah during a time of major world upheaval.

8) The personal requirements for an *'Ananias type'* ministry include being able to: -
8.1 Count the cost before starting out
8.2 Make a definite act of personal dedication
8.3 Minister to the most unlikely people
8.4 Be open to the correction of G-d's Holy Spirit
8.5 Re-think any previous flawed theology
8.6 Learn about Jewish life and customs
8.7 Take decisive action
8.8 Ask G-d to remove the veil of unbelief from His people

9) Saul was a typical case of a person who misused religion to escape the claims of Yeshua. Are we doing the same today with our Messianic activities? If so, all we are doing is trying to substitute our own righteousness for that already freely given by Yeshua through grace. We will repeat the mistake made by many of Yeshua's *'religious'* contemporaries, finding ourselves locked on the same suicide course as they were. The tragic developments marring both Jewish and Christian History would indicate that <u>religion is never more dangerous than when it becomes a means of running away from G-d.</u> The only remedy for this problem is repentance and a wholehearted faith in the Gospel which proclaims that, as a fully divine being, Yeshua became a Jewish man to die upon the cross and offer a perfect sacrifice for our sin. <u>Only through faith in Him is true righteousness to be found.</u> There are times when we should forget our religious background (whether Jewish or Christian) and focus our attention upon the Messiah. Only when we do this can we receive the discernment to pick out the best from our traditions.

Appendix 2: The Witness

(An Appeal to Open-Minded Jewish People to *'face the unthinkable'* concerning the Messiah)[25]

It is acknowledged that, given the long history of church-based anti-Semitism, the whole concept of witnessing about Yeshua is, by nature, both controversial and full of potential pitfalls. However, the following article hopes to witness to the gospel in such a way as to be more precisely tailored to the needs of Jewish people. I am neither a missionary nor a gospel preacher but, like every other adult believer in the Messiah, I too have a responsibility to witness to the truth should the opportunity arise.[26] As the following extract from Romans 10:14 states, "...how shall they believe in him of whom they have not heard?" I very much wish that mine will be a voice clearly heard by the Jewish people, a people for whom I have a genuinely strong concern. This makes it even more necessary to share the truth in the power of the Holy Spirit – to do less would display a shallow and worthless love on my part. However, should those reading these words not wish to hear the following (somewhat unusual) defence of the Messianic status of Yeshua then please, read no further! My intention is not to manipulate nor cajole people into hearing the message of salvation. Indeed, I take the view that this message is so good and so true that it can stand on its own merits without resorting to manipulation. The choice remains entirely with the reader.

A Society Meeting

During May 1978, when in the third year of a four-year Social Science degree course, I witnessed to a Reformed Jewish friend of mine who was on the same course. Through his good offices I had been able to attend meetings of the Jewish Society in February of that year. There, I'd encountered all sorts of Jewish People – rapidly learning that Orthodox Jews did not regard the Reformed as being *'properly Jewish,'* whereas the Reformed used to annoy the Orthodox by mimicking them. It took a formidable young matriarch (who was also the chairperson) to keep proceedings in some sort of order, at times openly cuffing the heads of the more disruptive members![27] However, when faced with the threat of anti-Zionism on the university campus this rather unruly gathering had promptly banded together into what appeared to be a remarkably strong unity and very quickly it was agreed what should be done to counter this threat. Later, over the Sabbath meal, I overheard one girl ask another of her male Orthodox peers how it was possible to obtain forgiveness of sins. His ready reply was *'repentance.'* I

---

[25] This work was first drafted in July 1999, slightly amended in March 2003 and finally reworked by late August 2007 with some minor revisions in July 2009 and October-November 2010.
[26] My main passion has been to guard the purity of Biblical doctrine in what has already become a spiritual *'Dark Age.'* I have no calling to be a full-time evangelist or missionary to the Jewish people.
[27] My subsequent engagement with Jewish people has tended to confirm that Orthodox Judaism places a particularly heavy burden upon its female members whose pivotal role is to preserve the family's Jewish identity.

thoroughly enjoyed the liveliness and intellectual stimulus provided by this group.

Cafeteria Conversation

Over the following few months, my Reformed Jewish friend – if not provoked to jealousy by my faith was certainly provoked to curiosity. I had a deep liking for him and his *'clownish'* sense of humour. The following conversation took place in a certain cafeteria and it was he who raised the question: -
"Do you really think that Isaiah 53 refers to Yeshua?"
"Yes, I do."
"But our Rabbis make it clear that it was referring to the whole of the Jewish people."
"That interpretation doesn't make sense as it clearly refers to an individual."
(A rather detailed discussion on this passage then followed).
"How could Yeshua be the Messiah when the Church has always been our worst enemy?"
(He then backed-up his case by referring to the Spanish Inquisition and other infamous examples of institutionalised Church persecution of the Jewish people)
I replied, *"But surely such examples show that the Christian view concerning the sinfulness of human nature is the correct one and if this is so, then people need G-d's salvation which only Yeshua can provide."*
(I knew then that the Spirit was present because I could argue with compassion.)
"You Christians have always been our enemies. There were the Crusades..." said with growing agitation.
"But they only show that Christ's warning about corruption in the Church was correct too."

The rest of the conversation went back and forth like this, with me stressing the need for faith in Christ and him saying, somewhat emotionally, that Christians had always hated Jews. Fearing that he was trying my patience (which he wasn't) he bought me an extra helping of ice cream after which he resumed his emotional outburst. I could see from the haunted and conflicting look in his eyes that he was both attracted to and repelled by the Messiah. Our intricate discussion ended, and we parted as friends. I saw him three months later at his home in London (I'd accepted some abortive job interviews there for civil service work). He pointed to his family tree, (hanging on a wall) which showed three Eastern European members who had died in 1941. My reaction to this was one of sadness; I could only stand quietly in silence. If my memory serves me correctly that was the last time I saw him, only later hearing that he had obtained a job as a Social Worker in the South East of England.

By 1999, (when this article was first being prepared for publication) I more fully accepted some of my friend's valid points concerning the behaviour of the Institutional Church. Apart from a few notable exceptions, my own abiding impression of English Christianity had become one of rudeness and stupidity.[28] Even when the Gospel of salvation had been clearly proclaimed it had gone largely unheeded or been totally ignored – with apathy dominating many a congregation. In response to such disinterest, many Church leaders have since tried to replace this message of salvation with their own human substitutes – inter-faith activity being just one example. I for one am ashamed at what the Church in this country has become, but the fact remains that, <u>to be ashamed of the Church is one thing, but to be ashamed of the Gospel is quite another.</u> Indeed, today's modern Church in the Western World has become a fulfilment of Christ's warning that, *"the love of many shall grow cold,"* (Matthew 24:12). Christ himself foresaw the degeneration of His Church and promised that, *"He who endures until the end shall be saved,"* (Matthew 24:3). Also, the mandate to provide a gospel witness to all nations will, of necessity, continue until *'the end'* comes. The decadence of the Church cannot, therefore, justify the view that states, *'The Church has done many dreadful things therefore it should also give up its gospel witness.'* Thankfully, each Christian's authority to share the gospel of life comes from Christ Himself and <u>not</u> from the Church. This means that any gospel witness should be conducted in as wise and as sensitive a manner as possible. Nowhere is this point more applicable than in relation to the Jewish people.

Dangerous Over-Optimism

Believers in the Messiah see Judaism, not as a bad faith, but rather as <u>the best possible religion people could have, apart from the revelation of the Messiah.</u> I can categorically state that building relationships with Jewish people has been one of the greatest and most enjoyable privileges of my life. I have found the Jewish sense of humour (displayed more often by the men) particularly endearing. In terms of ethics, mainstream Orthodox Judaism is admirable, in terms of scholarship, outstanding, and in terms of its many charitable activities thoroughly commendable. I have personally benefited from this faith in many, many ways and I feel very much at home in a Jewish atmosphere – more so than in many Churches. In contrast to much of the English Church, Orthodox Judaism has, at least, placed immense value upon learning and has followed the right moral principles. Also, as

---

[28] The comments made here are based upon the writer's own experiences of all the major strands of English Christianity, from 1975 until 2017.

well as my personal association with Judaism (with all its stimulating cultural activities) I have become familiar with some of the methods of Jewish Bible Interpretation,[29] which have since revolutionised my thinking by giving me insight into the various laws governing human behaviour. Both intellectually and personally, my contact with Orthodox Judaism had been one of profound enrichment.[30] I owe a great deal to that faith.

Unfortunately, getting to know G-d in a deeply personal way is not dependent upon having a *'good religion.'* The tragedy of Judaism (at least in its moderate Orthodox forms) is not that it is a bad or an evil religion (it isn't), but that it demonstrates the point that, <u>even the best of religions is never good enough to please G-d.</u> In His utter holiness, the Almighty Creator demands perfection from his creatures and sadly, no amount of religious practice can supply that perfection. Because I have grown up close to Judaism (having had links with it from my childhood) I can discern that, as a religious system, its central flaw has been (and still is) its hopelessly unrealistic and optimistic view of human nature. A typical representation of this flawed view is found on p. 142 of Rabbi Isidore Epstein's book, *'Judaism,'* which was first published in 1959. A very erudite (learned) man,[31] Epstein can justifiably be taken as a sound representative of the whole post-war Anglo-Jewish community. In the Penguin edition of his book, Epstein states that *"Judaism denies the existence of original sin needing a superhuman counterweight"* to that sin. After denying that Adam's sin brought about spiritual death to Mankind, Epstein smugly opines, *"Man can therefore achieve his own redemption by penitence, being assured that G-d himself is ever-ready in His abundance of loving-kindness to receive the penitent sinner and purge him of all iniquity."* In the previous paragraph he had airily dismissed *"some imaginary gulf between G-d and the World, or G-d and Man."*[32] His complacency about the human condition is almost obscene given the fact that it was made so recently after the Nazis' attempted genocide against Europe's Jewish population.

It needs to be stated clearly that Epstein's viewpoint contains the following doubtful assumptions: -
1) That the long-term effect of Adam's sin was confined only to the physical and not to the spiritual realm
2) That people can freely choose to get back into a relationship with G-d, through personal penitence
3) That obtaining a relationship with G-d does <u>not</u> require miraculous supernatural intervention

---

[29] A fuller discussion and application of these methods can be found in the writer's book, *'The Phantom Conflict.'*
[30] It's role in enriching *'Christian Reform Movements'* is examined by Newman (1925)
[31] He died in 1962 following a distinguished academic career
[32] Epstein p.143

4) That human penitence alone is enough to satisfy a totally holy G-d, who requires absolute perfection from His creatures

5) That the human sinful condition is insufficiently serious to require a divine saviour

His theology simultaneously flattered human nature and underestimated the awesome holiness of G-d. The mistake he made was very typical of rabbinic thinking.[33]

The evidence of Mankind's universal depravity (clearly seen throughout human history) would refute these assumptions. The Biblical evidence alone is damaging enough, with its vivid record of wars, atrocities and endless backslidings of G-d's people. However, in this last century, it must surely have been the *'Shoah,'* (meaning *'widespread disaster'* or *'destruction'*) which has provided the most powerful refutation of the traditional Jewish view of human nature. This sombre tragedy threw into cruel relief the divergence between Judaism's idealised view of human nature and actual harsh reality. If Epstein had wanted concrete evidence of the reality of the doctrine of original sin then the word *'Auschwitz'* should have been enough.[34] It was in such hellish places that human sinfulness reached its terrible zenith and the need for a supernatural redemption was brought sharply to the fore. Such overwhelming and stark evidence reduces Epstein's statements about human nature to nothing more than a faint whistling in the dark. Here was a man locked into that same kind of denial which had once caused Communist Party Officials to praise Stalin whilst being led out to be shot.

More generally, this over-optimism concerning human nature has served the Jewish community badly throughout the course of its history. It has led to what may be termed *'The Jewish Naivety.'* One example of this trait during the time of Christ's ministry, was the way many Jewish religious leaders, had been convinced that they could *'cut a deal'* with the power of Rome by offering a sacrifice for Caesar at the temple. (Their hope was to *'buy immunity'* from the requirement to worship Caesar's genius.) Like many such deceptions it seemed to work brilliantly for a time, but it did not, in the end, prevent Rome from brutally crushing the Jews after two failed revolts. This pattern was to be repeated in late Medieval Spain where Jewish Community leaders thought that a favoured position in the royal court as tax collectors would secure them immunity from the Inquisition. Also, in inter-war Germany many Jews stayed on in the misguided belief that they could *'ride out the storm.'* In its most recent manifestation, this naiveté about

---

[33] This is a point confirmed by many of the textual sources edited and translated by Alexander (1984)

[34] The writer would challenge any mature Jewish person to read Laurence Rees' (2005) book on Auschwitz and still deny the doctrine of innate human sinfulness.

human nature has figured greatly in the abortive Palestinian-Israeli peace process, (1993-2000). Once, when attending a public meeting in a certain Synagogue I challenged no less a personage than the Israeli Ambassador himself. I stated that, from the perspective of the Palestinian Liberation Organisation, this same *'peace process'* represented nothing more than a *'war by other means process.'* His somewhat vague reply was, to the effect, that all Israel could do was to hope. Later events would confirm that it was, once more, a case of *'whistling in the dark.'*

By the time of the sixtieth anniversary of Israel's foundation in May 2008, the murderous intentions of its enemies have become clear, yet there have remained elements within Israel's leadership who have continued to delude themselves into believing that land can be exchanged for peace. Such elements are as self-deceived as the community leaders of the Lodz and Warsaw Ghettoes who thought they could co-operate with the Nazis. As the frequent rocket attacks from Gaza indicate,[35] any *'land for peace deal'* would be a *'land for genocide deal.'* The fact is that, in the Middle East and elsewhere, the enemies of Israel have one simple aim in view; they want every Jewish person dead – preferably killed in the most degrading manner possible. It's naive to believe that there can ever be any appeasement of the irrational hatred which appears to dominate militant forms of anti-Semitism;[36] yet this misguided core view of human nature prevalent within mainstream Jewish Culture, is leading Israeli leaders to attempt just such an appeasement. They seem unable to acknowledge that anti-Semitism is an evil that never sleeps.[37]

At some definite point in the future (the exact timing of which G-d alone is aware) Judaism's inadequate view of human nature will prompt the Israeli nation to accept a global false messiah who will *'come in his own name'* (John 5:43). This Messiah is likely to gain acceptance amongst the Jewish people by seeming to be the answer to their desire for security[38] and by fulfilling their innate humanitarian idealism.[39] He will

---

[35] These were largely halted after Israel launched a ferocious military incursion into Gaza during December 2008. This was a move which sparked much international criticism and threats to try Israeli leaders as war criminals.

[36] In the writer's own experience anti-Semites can't be reasoned with. Their whole mentality is twisted and some of them delight in this hatred precisely because it is evil. An elderly survivor of Auschwitz confirmed these points in response to a question the writer asked him at a public meeting he attended on Tuesday, 27th January 2009.

[37] Well documented details of the current resurgence in anti-Semitism are provided by Melanie Phillips (2010) in her very perceptive book, *'The World Turned Upside Down.'*

[38] Their need for security is likely to be more keenly felt, should they have had to cope with yet another attempt to destroy them. The result of such an attempt would be to greatly increase their psychological suggestibility causing them out of desperation to accept any powerful figure viewed as guaranteeing their survival.

[39] An interview with the human-rights activist Rabbi Ascherman gave one example of idealistic humanitarianism relating to the present Middle Eastern Conflict, (Sunday Times

seduce their hearts by appealing to their best motives, even promising them an especially important *'humanitarian'* role in his New World Order. However, (again at a time of which G-d alone is aware) he will then suddenly turn upon the Jewish Nation, inflicting such great harm that they will once again face total annihilation. This whole scenario will be on a far bigger and more tragic scale than has ever been endured under previous false Messiahs like Bar Kocheba and Shabbethai Zvi (both of whom had beguiled the Jewish people after having gained a huge amount of support from influential Rabbis).[40] Judaism's optimism concerning human nature is again primed to be falsified in a most cruel and terrible way. The Jewish people will find that their naivety has, once more, placed them in great peril.

Sobering Evidence

For their own sake, Jewish people need to more seriously consider the sobering evidence of the last two thousand years. By a whole variety of persecutors (not all of them Christian) they *'have been driven from pillar to post.'* All too frequently, expulsion, fire and sword have been their lot; not to mention the wickedness of the Shoah and other cruelties perpetrated in the Modern Age. If nothing else, this tragic history should provide striking confirmation that humankind suffers from a perpetual, inborn tendency to do evil. People are not morally neutral agents, free to choose between a good and an evil principle. Indeed, the history of anti-Semitism would show that it is the evil principle which always triumphs in the soul of humanity. This is due to an inherent flaw within human nature itself. Sadly, overlooking this flaw has cost the Jewish people dearly – they keep on being surprised by the evil that afflicts them.

Such an appalling historical track record suggests that conventional Jewish thinking has got it badly wrong regarding human nature, and if it has been so wrong about human nature then it may also be wrong in its view of The Messiah? It is time for honest members of the Jewish community to begin facing the hitherto unthinkable possibility that Yeshua is indeed the Messiah. Regrettably, Bible prophecy appears to indicate that this will happen only when the Jewish people are once more, on the brink of annihilation. It is a time-worn custom for senior religious leaders (holding a prestigious position within their communities) to be singularly unreceptive to divine truth. Our Lord Himself found that such leaders were often the very last to *'face the unthinkable.'*[41] They had invested too much of their personal identity and public credibility in a failing religious system.

Magazine, 30th December 2007, P.58).
[40] Neither of these pseudo-Messiahs would have gained the momentum they did without the support of influential Rabbis and community leaders.

One of the signs of spiritual dysfunction within Judaism has been the practice of Cabbala Magic. A radio feature[42] (involving an interview with a certain Rabbi) confirmed that, by the late 1990s, this practice was enjoying something of a revival, especially amongst professionals and university people.[43] However, the programme seemed to put forward a dire health warning in relation to the practise of Cabbala magic. It appeared that it could unhinge the mind and blur the distinction between reality and fantasy. I have heard three independent members of the Jewish community give almost identical warnings. In contrast, the role of any true spiritual practice is to improve mental health – thereby placing people into a position where they can relate to G-d as sane and rational human beings. It should also help them to accept the reality of their sinfulness and their need for divine mercy. True spiritual practices help people *'face up to'* rather than *'escape from reality.'* If the spiritual practice in question persistently fails to do this, it is clearly spurious.

What Cabbala involves is an attempt to look for hidden codes in scripture through a variety of esoteric methods. It also seeks to control the supernatural through magical incantations and the employment of angelic names which also serve to release hidden spiritual energies within the practitioner. This is a blasphemous attempt to usurp a work that should belong exclusively to the deity – namely the controlling of angelic powers. With arrogant presumption, the Cabbalist tries to make himself into a *'mini-Lord of hosts,'* he (or she) having heeded the serpent's lie of Genesis 3:5c which promises, *"You shall be as G-ds, knowing good from evil."* By trying to assume divine powers the Cabbalist breaks the First Commandment, *"You shall have no other G-ds but me,"* (Deuteronomy 5:7). The practice of cabbalism commits a wretched betrayal of one of the most essential principles within Judaism. No wonder it can lead to insanity! The human psyche was never equipped to be a mini-G-d. Also, it is most improbable that Cabbala is authentically Jewish; its roots appearing to lie in a mixture of Babylonian magic, folk paganism and medieval philosophical speculation. Its origins are very murky, but as a fully developed system, Cabbala first arose in the thriving Jewish communities of medieval Spain around the year 1270.[44] However, incipient forms of Cabbalism

---

[41] In fairness, this stricture is even more applicable to Christian Church leaders whose spiritual blindness sometimes beggar's belief
[42] *'Sunday Today'* broadcast, Radio 4, Sunday 6 June 1999, (the revival in Cabbala practice it mentioned has continued)
[43] This feature also told of a large exhibition centred upon this very topic and on display at the Jewish Museum of London.
[44] Some of its meditative practices have strong affinities to Eastern Religion. This suggests that its world view may have been strongly influenced by Hinduism and was imported into Judaism via travelling Jewish merchants and the Sufi Orders of Islam. Such practices reflect a perspective that directly contradicts the world view of scripture which demands exclusive loyalty to the one true God. At its most basic philosophical level the Cabbala is opposed to Judaism. Its perspective owes more to the Hindu Swami (master of Yoga) and to the kind of sorcery practised by a Simon Magnus or Elymas (Acts 8:9-24

(with its invocation of angels) had existed centuries beforehand. It was roundly condemned in Colossians 2:18 (where mention is made of its ability to blend with early Christian heresies.) Practice of the Cabbala is a sign of spiritual emptiness which illustrates the following maxim: *'Where the Holy Spirit is absent magic abounds.'*[45] It represents one of Satan's *'substitutes'* for the true Messiah. Cabbalism's subterranean presence within Judaism also contradicts official rabbinical optimism concerning human nature. If people were as spiritually capable as Judaism makes them out to be then why should they feel the need to resort to the essentially pagan practice of Cabbala? Surely, penitence and obedience to the Law (Torah) would be enough?

In the long term, the revival of Cabbalistic practices will most probably lead to a considerable proportion of Jewish people becoming more receptive to the beguiling overtures of a false Messiah. Cabbalism will *'usher in'* this Messiah through its use of dreams, visions, lying signs and esoteric interpretations of scripture, (the latter lending everything an *'air of respectability'*). A whole plethora of these things will completely dwarf the supposed Cabbalistic miracles which accompanied the rise of Sabbethai Zvi. Cabbalism's main effect will be to increase psychological suggestibility, impressing its practitioners to override their reason and conscience and to go on to accept the emotional security a false Messiah will bring. The Cabbala will act as the driving force behind the Jewish Nation's near-total demise. In addition, influenced by a revival[46] in anti-Jewish *'conspiracy theory,'* (which will accuse the Jews of plotting to *'take over the world'* for their own nefarious purposes) other nations will think they are *'doing G-d a favour'* by ridding the earth of Judaism as a religion and culture.[47] The Jewish people will be a legitimate target for elimination because they will be viewed as *'not fitting in'* with the New World Order, (Esther 3:8). Thanks in part to the Cabbala the Jewish people will be in such grave peril that only direct intervention from G-d will rescue them. However, Cabbalism's seductive and disastrous influence will only be seen for what it is when Israel is on the brink of annihilation. Currently, it is the devil's tool to distract them from even considering the claims of the true Messiah.

& 13:4-12) than to the faith of the patriarchs and prophets.

[45] Since 2001, this point has been further illustrated by the huge popularity of fantasy books (and their subsequent films) and by role-playing PC games, some of which feature very overt forms of magic. The effect of this development has been to raise a whole generation steeped in hedonistic forms of neo-paganism, that's fundamentally antagonistic to Judaism and Christianity. By and large its members are closed to any idea of absolute truth. A vivid description of England's lapse into paganism is provided by Moreton (2010). He balances the more analytical approach of Campwell (2007).

[46] By January 2008, this revival was already happening in Arab nations and in countries like Iran where the president has pledged to *'wipe Israel off the map.'*

[47] In his book *'Voodoo Histories'* Aaronovitch (2009) repeatedly demonstrates how *'Conspiracy Theories'* may exercise a highly malicious influence in human affairs. The evidence he cites shows that they can take on a life of their own.

This innate naiveté concerning human nature constituted the major reason why the Jewish people had felt it impossible to accept the Messiah's ministry in the first place. After all (as Jewish thought goes), if we are not depraved sinners who can never please the Holy One then why do we need a saviour to die on our behalf? Yes, humanity needs divine help to make up for its various shortcomings, but people surely are not so bad as to need a divine saviour? Theirs is a religion based completely upon the wrong premise. Akin to every other religion (including false forms of Christianity like liberal Protestantism) Judaism has not sufficiently considered how sin dominates every aspect of the human condition. Sin is like an all-devouring cancer, burrowing its way into the deepest parts of our being. One reason why I became a Christian during the evening of Saturday, October 18th, 1975 was that it was the only Faith offering a realistic diagnosis of the human condition, (with all its corruption). It's still one reason why I continue to believe in Christianity – indeed a cynic would argue that, throughout its history the Church has worked rather too hard in trying to prove the doctrine of original sin!

Confronting the Unthinkable

Is it possible (even with divine help) that Jewish people should *'face the unthinkable,'* especially when they have endured long centuries of persecution and experienced profoundly agonising emotions? A genuine sense of empathy is needed and a full and frank acknowledgement that the Jewish people have been deeply wounded to the core of their being by all the ill treatment inflicted upon them by the Church.[48] So-called *'missionary work'* has also, over the years, been of an extremely insensitive nature. In July 1991, I was very nearly punched by a Messianic Jewish Missionary following a meeting in which he'd called some of his Jewish audience *'wolves.'*

I'm embarrassingly and painfully aware of the corruption of the Church – indeed it is one area in which I could lay claim to some degree of expertise.)[49] I too have been deeply distressed by those claiming to follow the Messiah and I can, to some extent, identify with the hurt experienced by an Orthodox Rabbi who compared the Church to a schoolyard bully. I've great empathy with my Reformed Jewish friend of some three decades earlier that'd been (quite rightly) defensive about the Church. However, to remain locked in this mental and emotional

---

[48] Only two nights before word-processing this point (on 28 April 1999) I heard an Orthodox Rabbi compare the behaviour of the Church to a schoolyard bully. Speaking to a mainly Roman Catholic audience one could only grieve over his sense of hurt.
[49] I would also admit to having a gift of being able to spot flaws within man-made religious systems. Despite causing trouble with church leaders, it's been a useful tool that has on occasion allowed reality to shine through.

attitude can never, in the long term, be a viable option. Hard facts need to be faced and the following series of questions help begin to do this: -

The first asks,
'Has the traditional Jewish view of human nature been true to what is known about human conduct – as revealed in Scripture and in its own Jewish history?'

The answer is *'No, it has not.'*

The second asks,
'Have the Rabbis (who are the leading representatives of Jewish thought) *adopted an over-optimistic view of human nature?'*

The answer is *'Yes, they have.'*

The third question asks,
'Has this over-optimistic view of human nature inflicted harm upon the Jewish community?'

Sadly, the answer is *'Yes, it has.'*

Finally,
'If, for all their great learning, the Rabbis have been wrong concerning human nature then could they also be wrong concerning Yeshua?'

The answer is *'Very likely.'*

By failing to accept the terrible reality of inborn human sinfulness, the rabbinic authorities (despite their many good points) have done themselves and their own community a considerable disservice. After all, why bother having a religion if one of its core elements is a refusal to accept some of the harsh realities concerning human nature?[50]

Taking the Initiative

If the Rabbinic view of human nature is wrong (and the many tragedies of Jewish history strongly indicate that it is) then the only way people can relate to the G-d of Israel is through some form of supernatural intervention. G-d must take the initiative in approaching people and not vice-versa. At this stage, the best candidate for that intervention is Yeshua of Nazareth. Only He fulfilled every promise made in Isaiah 53; only He brought large numbers of Gentiles into the worship of the Jewish G-d and only He can meet the deepest needs of sinful human

---

[50] This point is stated, not from any vantage point of superiority but because of the terrible realisation of my own sinfulness. The profound awfulness and depravity of sin should never be underestimated.

beings. It is time for the Jewish community to *'face the unthinkable'* by re-considering the Messianic claims of Yeshua of Nazareth. Should there be any Jewish person who has taken these points seriously to heart then my plea is that you put your faith in Him. Trust that He was sent by G-d to offer the one perfect blood sacrifice to provide a permanent atonement (*'covering'*) for your sin. Then believe that, by the power of his Holy Spirit, G-d raised Yeshua up from the dead three days after his crucifixion. Believe these things in your heart and mind and confess them with your mouth. Should faith be lacking then ask the G-d of your Forefathers to give it! The following prayer will help you make the required step of faith, (please read it through first before saying it). Above all, think carefully about what you are doing; except for the persuasion of your own conscience do not feel under any pressure to make this prayer. The freedom exists to ignore it.

G-d of Abraham, Isaac and Jacob,
G-d of Moses, Aaron and Joshua
G-d of Kings, Sages and Prophets,
G-d of all your people down the ages,
Their G-d, and my G-d,
Be faithful to your covenant promises
And remove any spiritual blindness from my mind concerning the Messiah.
Make my blind eyes see,
Allow my deaf ears to hear
And remove any hardness from my heart,
In your loving-kindness,
Regenerate me with your Holy Spirit
And grant me the strength to 'face the unthinkable.'
In your great mercy give me a true repentance that pleases you
And bestow the faith that will lead you to forgive my many sins

Lord G-d of Israel, please be merciful to me, a sinner,
All my good works are useless in your sight
For they cannot meet the perfect standards that your holiness demands
Consequently, I approach you in fear and trembling, as a lost sinner
In desperate need of a Saviour;
It is in this position of helpless dependence
That I ask you, Yeshua, to come into my heart and mind,
To fill my entire being with your gracious presence
By your grace (unmerited favour) I believe in you,
I trust that you were sent by G-d to die for my sin,
To pacify G-d's holy anger and to take the punishment I deserved,
Through the offering of your perfect blood sacrifice

Thanks to the faith given to me by your Holy Spirit
I believe, with all my heart, that Yeshua is Lord

And confess with my lips that G-d raised Him from the dead.
Thank you Yeshua for being my Lord and Saviour
Bless you for letting me know that the G-d of Israel
Is also my compassionate, Heavenly Father?
Please, by your Holy Spirit, show me what I should do
To follow-up this step of faith, Amen

Should you have made this prayer with any degree of faith then, *'Welcome into the Kingdom of G-d,'* for your new life has begun! Precisely how this new life will be worked out will take time, but for now it is sufficient that you rejoice and thank the Lord for his great mercies. The Book of Psalms would be a good starting point for such praise. Read some aloud and you may find that they've possibly taken on a fresh meaning, unknown to you before. In addition, take time to read such Gospels as *'Matthew'* and *'John'* and examine the more challenging *'Letters to the Romans'* and *'The Hebrews.'* These works have much to show about the Jewish basis of your new Faith.

For all of those who are already regenerate believers in the Messiah, my final exhortation is for you to ask yourself, *"Do I have a calling to pray for the Jewish people?"* If so, then pray that the *'scales will fall from their eyes'* and that they will receive the strength to recognise Yeshua as their Messiah which, for them, is to *'face the unthinkable.'* Also, pray that a faithful witness to the gospel will take place <u>before</u> the Jewish people undergo a further period of suffering. Should you continue praying for the Jewish people then G-d in His gracious mercy may confer some measure of divine blessing upon your life; this is because, when it comes to Israel and the Jews, powerful spiritual influences are at work. G-d is forever mindful of all the many promises He has made to restore them. He will not fail to vindicate those who, in one capacity or another, seek the welfare of His Ancient Covenant Nation. The G-d whom we follow keeps all the unconditional promises He has made in scripture. His Word is true, and his promises of blessing aimed specifically toward the Jewish people will come to pass.

Appendix 3: What Is Midrash?

*It should be stressed that in the various works consulted by the writer; the spelling of the key terms displayed some degree of variation. This is because they represent transliterations from the original **Hebrew**. Consequently, the spellings employed may only represent approximations to the wording used in the original terms.*

Section 1: Creed and Deed

This study will begin with a simple proverb devised by the writer:
No purity of doctrine means no purity of lifestyle and
The absence of right belief means the absence of right practice

Put simply, this proverb implies; *'no correct **Creed** means no correct deed.'* The doctrine of any true **Messianic** faith cannot be severed from their practical outworking. Faith and works are all part of the same package. To fully appreciate this, it is necessary to understand exactly what **Scripture** is saying. And it is here that three awkward questions arise: -
1) *"How is **Scripture** to be accurately interpreted?"*
2) *"How is it to be interpreted in such a way as to be free from all distorting cultural influences?"*
3) *"How can it to be interpreted in a manner that both honour's the **Lord** and his teaching as handed down by his **Apostles**?"*
In order to answer such questions it would prove useful to ask one more, namely; **"What is Midrash?"** The answer lies in the definition of the term **'Midrash'** itself and also in its origins within **Scripture**. A list showing the various forms of **Midrash** as used by the **Biblical** writers would also prove useful.

Briefly, **'Midrash'** refers to those methods of **Bible** interpretation employed by **Jesus** and the **Apostles** during the first century AD. It is derived from the **Hebrew** word **'Daresh,'** meaning *'to launch a thorough investigation'* or *'inquisitorial enquiry into something.'* It also has strong associations with such verbs as *'to interpret'* or *'to seek.'* Also present are connotations with the word *'urgency.'* The meaning of a passage is sought out in a mood of urgency rather than of casual interest. This is because **Scripture** itself is the very word of **God**. Consequently, **Midrash** simply means an urgent but rigorous, investigative interpretation into Divine revelation. As a discipline it is underpinned by the assumption that *any investigation into **God's** word could well be a matter of life or death.* If the results of that investigation are faulty, then the consequences could be truly devastating at the individual and wider corporate level.

However, the employment of the word **'Daresh'** in **2 Chronicle's 13:22** and **24:27** also indicates its association with the concept of *'story.'* Such a story may either be factual, (a record of historical events) or parabolic, (designed to illustrate a **Biblical** truth). Grasping either aspect is important because provides the key to seeing **Scripture** through First Century **Jewish** eyes. It certainly enables **God's** word to be interpreted in a more full and correct way.

Another noteworthy point is that, as a discipline, **Midrash** grew in complexity over the centuries. This meant that the **Midrashic** methods employed by a **medieval Rabbi** would not necessarily have been those of the First Century. This is because the **Medieval Rabbi** would have had to consider new challenges to his faith (most notably the presence of **Christianity** and **Islam**). Also **Jewish** scholarship itself continued to develop over the centuries and was responsive to fresh cultural influences (one of these being the rise of **Cabalistic** mysticism in the **Jewish** communities of medieval **Spain**). Interesting though such developments are, little can be said about them here for reasons of space. Instead the focus will only be on the first century **Midrash** of **Jesus** and the **Apostles**.

A second key word is *'hermeneutics'* – derived from the **Greek** word *'hermeneuo,'* meaning *'to interpret'* or *'to explain.'* It is employed in **John 1.38b** where the word *'Rabbi'* is translated into the **Greek Didaskalos** meaning *'master'* or *'teacher.'* Very simply, **Hermeneutics** can be defined as <u>the organised, methodical study and practice of **Bible** interpretation.</u> More specifically, it examines the merits and demerits of particular methods of interpretation. If **Midrash** is more concerned with ascertaining *"What does **God's** word really say about a particular topic?"* Then **Hermeneutics'** focus is upon resolving the question *"How can **God's** word be best interpreted?"* However, despite this difference in emphasis **Midrash** is an integral part of **Bible Hermeneutics**. After a long period of neglect within the **Gentile Church Midrash** is becoming an increasingly important discipline – of great practical value to the **Church** today.

Section 2: The Forms of Midrash

As an approach to **Scripture**, **Midrash** exists in various forms. In order of growing complexity these are: -

1) Basic (or Simple) Midrash

This represents the simplest type of **Midrash** consisting of: -
a. A short quotation from **Scripture**.
b. Followed by a brief *'running commentary'* that usually concentrates upon the literal meaning of the short quotation.
c. This in turn is then followed by another brief quotation (or quotations) from other passages of **Scripture**.
d. Another running commentary (or set of commentaries) accompanies this other quotation (or quotations). Once again, attention is usually only given to the literal meaning.

e. Lastly, a concluding sentence (or quotation) may be used in order to sum up the main theme.

A **Basic Midrash** can either long or short. One example of a simple **Midrash** is found in **Hebrews 2.**

2) Comparative Midrash

In this instance, two or three complementary **Bible** passages are brought together in order to shed greater light upon one main topic or theme. The passages used to do this may vary in length from a few paraphrased verses to whole Books. One particular example of a **comparative Midrash** can be found in **Hebrews 7** where **Genesis 14:17-20** and **Psalm 110:4** are brought together in order to highlight **Christ's** eternal Priesthood.

3) Contextual Midrash

This **Midrash** examines the context of a particular **Bible** passage in order to obtain its true meaning. Attention is paid to the author of the passage and to its historical and **Spiritual** background. A particular example of a **Contextual Midrash** occurs in **Galatians 3:17** where **Paul** shows that the **Mosaic Law** came *"Four hundred and thirty years after"* **Abraham.**

4) Creedal (or Doctrinal) Midrash:

Greatly varying in length, this particular form of **Midrash** attempts to logically arrange **Biblical** teaching by setting it out in concise summary form. This is achieved in such a way that the connections existing between individual doctrines can be clearly seen. Often used to assist worship and rote learning, **Creedal Midrash** follows a set structure in which there is: -
a. A sudden break in the immediately preceding statement.
b. Formalised instruction, briefly summarising key **Biblical** truths.
c. A logical arrangement of doctrines.
d. A total absence of any visual imagery.
e. A sudden, at times, almost abrupt ending.
f. A brief commentary (or exhortation) seeking to elucidate key points and to show how any formal instruction may be applied in daily life.
Of especial note, is the clear distinction made between the more authoritative formalised teaching and the practical moral instruction surrounding it. Moreover, in terms of layout there is some resemblance to the early **Creeds** of the **Church**. Strongly reinforced is the possibility that these early statements of faith originated in first century **Messianic Judaism** rather than in third or fourth century **Greek Hellenism.** A particular example of this **Midrash** can be found in **Ephesians 1:3f** and also in **Colossians 1:15-23.**

5) Exempla Midrash

Here, the lives of those who died long ago are brought into focus and interpreted in a moralistic way having practical implications for those still living. Popular in **Hellenistic Judaism,** this type of **Midrash** assumes a structure where there is: -
a. The statement of a theme.
b. Selected persons are introduced who, by their lives help to illustrate that theme.
c. After a brief re-cap of the main theme a practical application is given.
A particular example of this **Midrash** is found in **Hebrews 11:1-12:13.**

6) Exodium (or Proem) Midrash

This **Midrash** forms a rhetorical, near poetical prologue, outlining the major themes of a literary work in a forceful and direct manner. Often marking a dramatic start to a work its main purpose is to attract the attention of the reader. A particular example of This **Midrash** is found in **John 1:1-18** (and also in **Hebrews 1:1-4**).

7) Homiletic Midrash:

This **Midrash** offers simple doctrinal instruction by using a four-part structure comprising: -
a. An introductory formula e.g. *'as it is written.'*
b. A **Harez** (or *'pearl stringing'*) of a diverse collection of **Bible** passages; all gathered together in order to illustrate a key theme.
c. A commentary showing how this collection of **Bible** passages confirms and explains the major theme under scrutiny.
d. A final conclusion made to sum up key points and to encourage practical application.
A particular example of this **Midrash** can be found in **Romans 3:9-20.**

8) Parabolic Midrash:

This **Midrash** hopes to convey divinely revealed truth through the employment of vivid stories (parables), designed to gain the hearer's attention and to help him deal with **Spiritual** realities. It is mainly used with uneducated audiences who think visually, *i.e.* in picture terms. **Parabolic Midrash** often follows a definite structure comprising of: -
a. A brief introductory phrase e.g. *'Hear another parable.'*
b. A short, vivid story employing situations from daily life in order to illustrate **one** particular point. Sometimes a note of humour is struck; especially when hypocrisy is being exposed.
c. A building up to a sudden, often surprising climax, designed to provoke thought and to challenge any **sinful** attitudes.

d. An interpretation of the story, or the beginning of a *'question and answer'* dialogue. Sometimes, a brief concluding comment or a direct *'lead in'* to more formalised methods of **Bible** interpretation may be added. In contrast to allegories (where every detail may have significance) parables try only to convey one single point; three examples of this **Midrash** are found in **Matthew 21:28-22:14.**

9) Parishiyot Midrash

This more complex form of **Midrash** endeavours to resolve apparent contradictions in **Scripture** by using a definite structure that sets out to provide: -
a. An introduction to the main theme.
b. The employment of a standard introductory phrase at key points *e.g. 'it is contained in the Scripture.'*
c. The **Petkah** (or base passage) followed by a running commentary.
d. An opposing intersecting (apparently contradictory) **Bible** passage with a running commentary.
e. A final concluding (or reconciling) passage followed by a brief commentary resolving the apparent contradiction.

Often a **Parishiyot Midrash** may occur a number of times in order to resolve a whole series of problems. Sadly, over the centuries it has, as a technique, become seriously under-used in ecclesiastical **theology**. Its absence has perhaps contributed to an unnecessary prolongation of various doctrinal controversies. One possible example of such an unnecessary prolongation has been the long dispute over *'free will'* and *'predestination.'* A particular example of a **Parishiyot Midrash** can be found in **I Peter 2:4-10.**

10) Peshar Midrash

This too is a more complex form of **Midrash** comprising of: -
a. A main, (sometimes lengthy or paraphrased) **Bible** quotation.
b. An **exegesis** (simple exposition) usually including: -
- Smaller re-quotes from the main passage.
- Quotations from other **Scriptural** passages used to apply **Deuteronomy 19:15** and to reinforce the main line of argument.
- A practical application that may also include re-quotations and other **Biblical** material.

Throughout the main quotations the use of paraphrasing may denote the use of **remez,** (*'hinting'*). Here, only a few words, (sometimes the opening and closing words) of a passage are taken to encompass everything contained within that passage. The cry of dereliction in **Matthew 27:46** is one example. Here **Christ** quotes the opening words of **Psalm 22,** thereby implying that the whole of **Psalm 22** was applicable to Him. Similarly, the paraphrase of **Genesis 14:17-20** in **Hebrews 7:1-2** would have allowed for contemporary **Jewish** readers to realise that the whole of **Genesis 14:17-20** was under review. A particular example of **Peshar Midrash** can be found in **Hebrews 3:1-4:11** (and also in **7:1-8:5**).

11) Rez-Peshar Midrash

Often integrated within other forms of **Midrash**, this particular approach attempts to interpret sacred mysteries and locate the fulfilment of particular prophecies through the employment of **Rez-Peshar** [mystery interpretation]. It employs the *'this [occurrence] is that [fulfilment of a prophecy]'* formula. The **Apostle Peter** employed it with great effect when (in **Acts 2:16**) he states, "*But this is that which was spoken by the prophet Joel.*" Clearly based upon the assumption that **God's** Word *'the Scriptures cannot be broken'* (**John 10:35b**), **Rez-Peshar** is dependent upon the belief that all unconditional **Bible** prophecies can have a number of literal fulfilments, often separated by long interludes of time. The *'this is that'* formula is a tool to finding such fulfilments. It does this by comparing the behaviour of social and religious actors from the different time periods. If strong similarities exist their behaviour this formula can be used. The writer managed to apply it when he uncovered strong similarities in the behaviour of senior **Anglican Clergy** and the temple priesthood in **Jeremiah's** time. Although useful in relating contemporary events to divine revelation, **Rez-Peshar** can suffer from two drawbacks. Firstly, it is a somewhat blunt instrument that cannot by itself distinguish between a fulfilment of prophecy and a final, complete fulfilment which may only take place immediately prior to the **Messiah's** return. Secondly, it is not an appropriate tool to employ with prophecies (such as **Isaiah 52:13-53:1f**) which themselves were totally fulfilled at the **Messiah's** first coming. It should be used with caution when relating **Scripture** to contemporary affairs. A particular example of **Rez-Peshar Midrash** can be found in **Matthew 3:3a** (and also in **Luke 4:21**).

12) Typological Midrash

This is possibly the most complex form of **Midrash,** which assumes that past occurrences (events, institutions and personages) can have something to say about present day and future occurrences. Such occurrences may also have something to say about developments in the **Spiritual** realm. In order to uncover the fulfilment of past prophecies recourse may be made to the **Rez-Peshar**, (*'this is that formula'*). The following three forms of **Typology** constitute this particular **Midrash**: -

a. Historical (or Horizontal) Typology

Here past occurrences (called **types**) are seen as prophetic foreshadows anticipating present day and future occurrences (known as **anti-types**). For example, with regard to the first temple the **Rez-Peshar** formula can be employed to state: *'this building (**type**) is that anticipation of the **Church** and the millennial temple (present and future **anti-types**).'* Such an example shows that this *'type'* can anticipate a number of *'anti-types.'* Alternatively, it would be possible to say that *'this modern **Gentile Church** (**anti-type**) is that particular fulfilment of the **Laodocean Church** (**type**) mentioned in **Revelation 3:14f**).'* As these two examples show, the **Rez-Peshar** formula can either begin with a *'type'* or an *'anti-type.'*

b. Spiritual (or Vertical) Typology

Employed is a **Mashal/Nimshal** Formula (seen often in parables) where physical reality (the **Mashal**) is assumed to speak about **Spiritual** reality (the **Nimshal**). For example, when the moon is darkened in **Isaiah 13:10** (and in **Matthew 24:29**) it is a sign of darkness covering the nations. Also, any reddish colour is symbolic of large-scale martyrdom where the blood of the **saints** will be freely shed. More specifically, a **Rez-peshar** formula could highlight this point by saying *'this darkening of the moon near the Passover (the **Mashal**) is that growing **Spiritual** darkness of the nations under the World-wide government of **anti-Christ** (the **Nimshal**).'* Alternatively, *'this darkness of the nations (the **Nimshal**) is reflected by that darkening of the moon (the **Mashal**).'* These two examples confirm that the **Rez-Peshar** formula can begin with either the ***'Mashal'*** or ***'Nimshal.'***

C. Synchronised (Or Combined) Typology

This **typology** takes place when the previous two typologies are combined within the same occurrence. A **synchronised typology** occurs with regard to the crucifixion, which was simultaneously:
- *A Type,* pointing forward to the various forms of suffering (crucifixion) every faithful believer would have to undergo.
- *An Anti-Type,* pointing backward, by fulfilling specific **Bible** prophecies and **Mosaic** rituals, *e.g.* the Day of **Atonement** in **Leviticus 16**.
- *A Mashal,* pointing upwards to the darkness covering the land conveying the physical expression of separation from Divine blessing.
- *A Nimshal,* pointing downwards to the terrible Spiritual reality of hell, where like **Jesus** on the cross, people will be tormented by a raging, thirst **(Luke 16:24 and John 19:28).**

As with the previous two typologies the **Rez-Peshar** formula may also be used.

When employing a **typological midrash**, great care must be taken to draw a clear distinction between **typology** and **allegory.** In allegory, the story is viewed as containing *'hidden truths'* not available for normal believers. (Allegories are rarely used in **Biblical** literature and can be viewed as a narrative or a story containing a whole array of hidden, underlying truths – known as the **Sensus Plenior**.) This stance can pave the way for a dangerous form of elitism. Where it occurs, one has a passive congregation relying upon an infallible *'Anointed'* teacher to interpret **Scripture** for them. Moreover, no form of **Typology** should ever be used to establish Doctrine. Rather **typology's** role is only to illustrate those truths, which have already been elicited from the literal interpretation of easily understood **Bible** passages. The plain meaning of those passages should be clear to all people of good will. A particular example of a **Typological Midrash** can be found in **Hebrews 9:23** where the earthly tabernacle is regarded as built in *'the pattern of things in the heavens.'* Incidentally, **Typological Midrash** is built upon the assumption that there are regular patterns of behaviour to be seen in **God**, man and Satan alike. A keen and thorough of those patterns should help devout believers to interpret both **Scripture** and the social environment in which they live.

All twelve forms of **Midrash** can be combined to form a **Versatile Midrash** which occurs when more than one form of **Midrash** is employed within the same piece of teaching. A particular example of Versatile **Midrash** is provided in the book of **Hebrews**, which makes use of most of the previously described forms of **Midrash**.

Section 3: The Principles of Midrash

In the previous chapter it was shown that **Midrash** was a discipline embracing a number of other disciplines including ethics, history, linguistics, sociology and **theology**. Also implied was the possibility that **Midrash** contained various principles of interpretation and that these principles were employed by **Jesus,** the **Apostles** and virtually all of those who wrote what came to be known as the *'New Testament.'* It is these principles, which form the central focus of this study. However, before looking at them, it is first of all necessary to make a few introductory comments. These will be presented as an **Exodium** or *'Proem'* **Midrash** as follows:
*In his wisdom The **Lord**,*
*When he inspired his **Scriptures***
*Through his **Spirit** of Holiness,*
Not only gave out His Word
But in his mercy
He also gave out the means
To interpret that Word
So believers
From Jewish and Gentile backgrounds alike
Could grow in grace and display
*The fruit of **God's Spirit***
*As found listed in **Galatians 5:22-23***
It therefore obliges every believer,
On the strength them to: -
Rightly divide the word of truth.' **(2 Timothy 2:15)**

Through employing
Those means of interpretation,
That **Scripture** *itself*
Has ordained.
By so doing,
They themselves should avoid
Much error and grow into a fuller
Understanding of the truth
Thus, in time,
They should grow
To resemble their Messiah
The **Saviour**
Whom they follow

In simple, near poetical language this **Exodium** has summed up why it is important for believers to both learn and to practise the principles of **Midrash**. The success of any **Bible** interpretation can be practically assessed by the degree of holiness it has helped to produce in the believer's life.

Within the discipline of **Midrash** there exists, various forms of **Bible** interpretation or **Middot** (meaning *'method'* or *'principle.'*) Only a selection will be described here. However, **Rabbi Hillel** (who ministered around the time of **Jesus '** birth) or his immediate predecessors had already outlined the first seven **Middots**. These principles were: -

1) Qalva-Hama

That which applies in a **less** *important case will also apply in a* **more** *important case.*

This principle originated in **Genesis 44:8, Exodus 6:12, Deuteronomy 31:21, 1 Samuel 23:3 Jeremiah 12:5, Ezekiel 15:5, Proverbs 11:3** and **Esther 9:2**. It was used by **Jesus** in **Matthew 7:11, 10:2 Mark 2:25-28** and **Luke 12:28** – and by **Paul** in **Romans 5:12-21**.

2) Gezerah-Shavah

Similar phrases or behaviour recorded in two or more different passages **mean the same** <u>thing</u> *and can be interpreted in* **the same way.**

For example, the word **'Be-mo Ado'** (meaning *'in its appointed time.'*) Is used both in regard to the Paschal Lamb **(Numbers 9:2)** and the **Tamid** or perpetual offering **(Numbers 28:2)**. From this fact, it is possible to deduce that the Paschal lamb can be offered on the Sabbath as well as the **Tamid**. To prevent arbitrary interpretations arising from this logical **Middot** a **Gezerah-Shavah** can only be advanced if: -

a. It is already present in tradition.
b. Both passages come from the **Pentateuch.**
c. The two words must not only be similar but must also be found in a similar context. The two previously cited verses from Numbers occur in the context of making offerings to the **Lord.** In **Romans 4:1-12 Paul**, in a somewhat loose way used the same rule when he joined together **Genesis 15:6** and **Psalm 32:1.**

3) Binyan 'Ad Mi-Katuv' Ehad

The <u>same considerations</u> apply when the <u>same phrase</u> is present in a number of texts.

In this method the word construction or **Binyan** acts as a basis to a number of conclusions *i.e.* if work could be done on the Sabbath to gain necessary food, it could also be done on other religious feasts as well. More specifically, in **Leviticus 17:13** it is possible to see that the **Binyan** is that pouring out of the blood by the hand. This word construction acts as the basis for the conclusion that the covering of any blood accidentally spilt on the ground must be done by the hand and not by the foot. In this way, relating two texts together and then applying the outcome to other passages could establish a teaching. However, on occasion a principle can be established based solely upon one passage, especially so if the passage concerned a legal ruling given in the **Pentateuch.**

4) Kelat U-Ferat:

*A general principle can be **qualified by** a specific rule <u>or</u> a specific rule can be **extended into** a general principle.*

In **Leviticus 1:2**, the term *'cattle'* is restricted by the word *'herd'* which rules out non-domesticated cattle, although in normal usage *'cattle'* covers both domesticated and non-domesticated animals. In **Mark 12:30-31 Jesus** turned two great commands to love **God (Deuteronomy 6:4-5)** and to love one's neighbour **(Leviticus 19:18)** into general principles. By doing so he ruled out the popular **Zealot** teaching that it was right to hate one's enemies **(Matthew 5:43).**

5) Perat U-Kheln

*General principles determine **specific** interpretations.*

In **Exodus 22:9.** the word *'beast'* includes other animals beyond those specifically mentioned. In **1 John 2:10,** love for one's brother should go on to encompass love for one's neighbours and even one's enemies.

6) Ka-Yose Bo Be-Maqom 'Aher

*A difficulty in one text can be resolved by comparing it to another **simpler** text that contains similar subject matter, if not wording.*

The apparent lukewarm stance taken toward **Spiritual** gifts in **1 Corinthians 13:8-10** can be resolved by referring to **1 Corinthians 14:1.** This plainly teaches believers to *'desire **Spiritual** gifts'* like prophecy. In addition, one could also refer to **1 Thessalonians 5:19-21** which teaches them to *'prove'* but not to *'despise'* such *'prophesying.'*

7) Daviar Ha-Lamed Me-'Inyano

*Allow the **context** to establish the **meaning** and **application** of a particular passage.*

Paul used this rule (in **Romans 4:10**), when he stressed that the physical context of **Abraham's** justification by faith was one wherein circumcision had not yet been introduced. In **Galatians 3:17** the historical context was some **430 years** <u>before</u> the Law came into being. This principle is important because it can help prevent arbitrary interpretations of **God's** word. Acknowledged is the saying that states: *'A text without a context is a pretext.'*

8) Shene Khiuum Ha-Makhhisim Zet Et Zeh Ad She Yavo Ha-Katuv Ha-Shelichi Ve-Yak A Beineihem

Two *apparently **contradictory** texts can be reconciled by a **<u>third</u> reconciling** text.*

Useful in religious controversies and helpful in resolving doubts; one example can be provided from the following three verses:
a. Proverbs 26:4, *(The **contradicted** text)* this warns, *"**Answer <u>not</u>** a fool in his folly lest you be like unto him."*
b. Proverbs 26:5, *(The **contradictory** text)* this exhorts, *"**Answer** a fool in according to his folly lest he be wise in his own conceit."*
c. Ecclesiastes 3:1, *(The **reconciling** verse)* this counsel's people to remember that: *"To everything **there is a season** and a time to **every** person under heaven."*

In other words, there are times when it is right not to rebuke a fool and times when it is right to rebuke him. People need to know **God's** will in a particular situation.

Other more specific kinds of **Middot** may be used. These include:

(I) Al Tikrei

*Do **not** read this but read that meaning of a text.*

A particular meaning maybe amplified, by replacing a word within a text with one that sounds similar but has an added or updated meaning. **Hebrews 2:7** replaces the word *'God'* in **Psalm 8:5** with the word *'angel.'* Presumably this is done in order to stress Man's humble state. Obviously, this particular technique can be open to the kind of serious abuse of **Scripture** as seen in the cults. Hence, it is always wise to put any such changes in brackets beside the original word in the text. A case in point is the **Shema** whose original meaning is brought out by the bracketed insertion *"Hear o **Israel** the **Lord** our **God** is [the Pluralistic] one **Lord**."*

(II) Ein Mikra Yoze Mi-Ydei Feshuto

*A **Biblical** passage **never** loses its **plain** meaning regardless of any additional, **allegorical** or **Typological** interpretation.*

A case was **Jesus'** own **Typological** interpretation of the raised serpent in **John 3:14.** He did not rob **Numbers 21:9** of its historical meaning – both levels of meaning could co-exist together.

(III) Gematria

*The numerical values of names or phrases **may** reveal something about their character.*

Echoes of this technique may exist in **Revelation 13:18** where, in the **Hebrew,** the letters of **Nero Caesar** add up to *'God.'* In addition, **'666'** also symbolises **sinful** incompleteness. The name for **Abraham's** servant **Eliezer** in the **Hebrew** has a value of **318,** which equalled the number of soldiers **Abraham** sent out to battle **(Genesis 14:14).** Implied here is the possibility that much of his life was a battle!

(IV) Hedqeth

*Allegories can **only** reinforce but **not** determine a particular teaching or doctrinal issue.*

This limitation occurs in **Galatians 4:22f** where the two wives of **Abraham** were treated as an allegory for the **Old** and **New Covenants**. A variation of this **Middot** employs arguments from **Typology**. Two instances of this approach occur in **Matthew 12:40,** (where **Jesus** saw **Jonah's** experience as typifying his own) and **Matthew 24:37,** (where the corrupt days of **Noah** typify the **World** before the Second Coming). **Paul** himself frequently employed **Scripture Typologically** – most notably in **Romans 5:12-21, 1 Corinthians 10:1-11** and **Galatians 3:10-12.** Particularly interesting is **1 Corinthians 10:1-11** where certain events in **Israel's** wilderness wanderings were seen as foreshadowing judgement upon those who abused the **Lord's** supper. Another case is **1 John 1:11-15** where the hatred of **Cain** for his brother in **Genesis 4:1-9** typifies the hatred of the **World** for **God's** people.

However, at this point it is necessary to emphasise that doctrine cannot under any circumstances be built upon either **allegory** or **typology**. Rather, any true teaching can only be established by referring to the plain, literal meaning of easy to understand passages whose contexts have been fully considered. **Allegory** and **typology** can be used to illuminate or strengthen the credibility of a particular doctrine. Under no circumstances can they be used as a basis for creating doctrine. Any failure to heed this principle can very quickly lead to error.

(V) Nekuddat,

Dots, the position of dots over certain letters can call to attention some noteworthy features.

Genesis 33:4, the position of the dots in confirmed that **Jacob's** kiss from **Esau** denoted a sincere reconciliation. **Jesus** himself stressed the importance of **Nekuddat** in **Matthew 5:18.** Even the tiniest marks on the **Bible** manuscript were viewed as having a **Spiritual** significance.

(VI) Notariqum

Words and names can be treated as character revealing acronyms.

The name **Jacob** means *'trickster'* or *'cheat'* whilst **Jesus** **(Yeshua)** means *'the **Lord** saves.'* Basically, the assumption was that if you had the name, you also had the character. This fact explains **Jabez's** anguish in **1 Chronicles 4:9-10,** for in the original **Hebrew** his name means *'pain'* or *'sorrow.'* He was quite naturally desperate not to live up to it.

(VII) Semukhim

*A conclusion based upon the juxtaposition of a **number** of verses.*

Presumably, this **Middot** was used in order to establish a case on the basis of more than one witness **(Deuteronomy 19:15). Paul** used this method with great effect in **Romans 3:10-20** – where he established his **Biblical** witnesses before arguing his case for the universal guilt of humanity.

(VIII) The Distinction Between Halakah And Haggadah

Halakah *legal texts are* **more** *authoritative than* **Haggadah** *non-legal, devotional or historical texts and should therefore carry greater weight in any disputed interpretation.*

First century **Judaism** and the early **Church** were largely agreed that **Halakah** should be interpreted more cautiously – with only the plain, literal meaning being followed. Any **allegorical** or **Typological** interpretations were barely present. **Jesus** himself adopted a very strict, literal interpretation of **Deuteronomy 24:1** when debating the issue of divorce in **Matthew 19:3-12** and **Mark 10:2-12. Paul** also preserved this distinction when he quite *'literally'* interpreted ethical commands such as **Leviticus 19:18 (Romans 13:9** and **Galatians 5:14).** Overall, it does appear that the resolute veneration for **Torah,** which prevailed in first Century **Judaism** acted as a check on more fanciful methods of interpretation being applied to **Halakah.** The text was viewed as being too sacred for any kind of manipulation or playful human speculation.

What has emerged from this analysis into the principles of **Midrash** has been the versatility of the **New Testament** writers when employing **Middot.** Whilst not being over-rigid in their application of it, they made use **midrash** principles whenever they saw fit in order to deliver divine truths to needy people. Their particular contribution was to add a **Christological** emphasis so that **Midrash** became a means whereby attention focussed upon the one true **Messiah** to whom the **Scriptures** testified. Their continued use of a tried and trusted method of interpretation greatly reduced the risk of **Scripture** becoming a playground for human speculation whilst enabling it to act as a source of life. This already existing **Hermeneutic** tradition was taken up and used under the direction of the **Holy Spirit** for a sacred purpose. As a result, many ancient **Jewish** techniques of interpretation became the **Scripture's** own techniques of interpretation. Therefore it is possible to defend most of the methods listed in this article on the grounds that they represent authentically **Biblical** (as well as **Ancient Jewish**) guidelines for opening up the Word of **God.** It is to their own considerable peril that modern **Christians** dismiss or neglect those methods. These methods are just as readily applicable to **Messianic Jews** who wish to recover the genuine **Hebraic** roots of their faith.

Section 4: The Practice of Midrash

Rightly interpreting **God's Word** is both a joy and a challenge. It is a practice that every believer must learn to actively avoid that mental passivity, which often acts as a doorway to error. The methods of interpretation can be understood and used by most literate lay people, having the willingness and ability to learn. This section contains examples of the simpler forms of **Midrash**. Following these, some practical advice is given on what may be termed **'DIY'** *('Do it yourself')* **Midrash**. However, it must be clearly understood that all *'DIY Midrash'* must adhere to the principles of sound **Biblical** interpretation (as listed in the previous chapter). Should any departure take place from this, it would act as a clear sign that the Word of **God** was being mishandled – possibly to a person's own eternal destruction **(2 Peter 3:16)**. Bearing such constraints in mind, it is now possible to forge ahead and show how to construct a basic **Midrash**.

One advantage of any *'DIY Midrash'* is that it requires only a few practical resources other than a **Bible** (preferably containing cross references), a Concordance – with **Cruden's**, **Strong's** and **Young's** being very good sources to refer to. (A possibly a simple textbook on **theology** may also help) Once these resources have been gathered take note of the following guidelines: -
1) Begin with the simpler forms of **Midrash** <u>before</u> working up to the more complex forms.
2) Clearly sum up (preferably in one sentence) the area to be examined *e.g. "Divine guidance in the believer's life."*
3) Employ a concordance or **theological** textbook to look up appropriate headings, *e.g. 'guide'* or *'guidance.'* Take careful note of any relevant **Scripture** passages pertaining to these headings.
4) Make a note of those **Scriptures**, which clearly refer to the subject in hand. Disregard those that seem ambiguous or obviously refer to something else.
5) Prayerfully note down the **theological** and practical points which appear to emerge from these passages. Also record the way in which they could be applied to daily life.
6) Arrange all relevant citations, quotations and written points into an appropriate **Midrash** structure.
7) Begin applying those points whilst referring back to the **Midrash** structure for further clarification and to help monitor progress. Neater improved versions of the original **Midrash** may be created.

It should be possible, at this stage to see that the outworking of **Midrash** can have many practical benefits in daily living. After all, it is **Yahweh's**

Holy Word that is being dealt with, and **not** some esoteric piece or technical knowledge, available only to specifically qualified people. In this context it can be seen that **Midrash** is a discipline **not** just for the expert, but something that can benefit **all** **Spiritually** minded believers. Also, **Midrash** is best learnt through practice!

Some of the beneficial results of **'DIY Midrash'** can be seen in the following **Homiletic Midrash** on divine guidance. Relevant **Bible** passages were obtained by looking up the word *'guide'* or *'guided'* in various **Concordances**. For ease of reference, this **Midrash** has been placed in clearly distinguished sections with appropriate subheadings.

A *'DIY Midrash'* On Divine Guidance

Statement of The Main Theme

The main theme of this particular **Midrash** is that of divine guidance in the life of the believer.

Introductory Formula

"As it is written"

Haraz *(i.e. 'the stringing together' of relevant passages)*

1) *"You in your mercy have* led forth *the people which you have redeemed: You have guided them in your strength unto your holy habitation,"* **(Exodus 15:13)**

2) *"For the* **Lord** knows the way *of the righteous,"* **(Psalm 1:6a)**

3) *"As for* **God***, His way is perfect: the word of the* **Lord** *is tried: He is a buckler to* all *that trust Him,"* **(Psalm 18:30)**

4) *"The* **Lord** is *my shepherd: I shall* not *want."* **(Psalm 23:1)**

5) *"Commit your way unto the* **Lord***: trust also in Him: and He shall bring it to pass: He will be* our guide *even unto death,"* **(Psalm 37:5 & 48:14b)**

6) *"You* shall guide me *with your counsel and afterward receive me to glory,"* **(Psalm 73:24)**

7) *"But made His own people to go forth like sheep and* guided them *in the wilderness like the flock,"* **(Psalm 78:52)**

8) *"He* keeps *the paths of judgement and* preserves *the way of the* **Saints***,"* **(Proverbs 2:8)**

9) *"I am the* **Lord** *Your* **God** *which teaches you to profit, which leads [guides] you by the way you should go,"* **(Isaiah 48:17b)**

10) *"For He that has mercy on them [His people] shall lead [guide] them, even by the springs of water shall He guide them,"* **(Isaiah 49:10b)**

11) *"And the* **Lord** *shall guide you continually and satisfy your soul in drought, and make fat your bones,"* **(Isaiah 58:11)**

12) *"Take no [anxious, fretful] thought for the morrow, for the morrow shall take thought for the things of itself. Sufficient unto the day is the* **evil** *thereof,"* **(Matthew 6:34)**

13) *[He] "guides our feet into the way of peace,"* **(Luke 1:79b)**

14) *"And the sheep hear His voice: and He calls His own sheep by name, and leads [guides] them out,"* **(John 10:3)**

15) *"I am the good shepherd [who] gives His life for the sheep,"* **(John 10:11)**

16) *"When He the* **Spirit** *of truth is come, He will guide you into all truth: for what He shall hear that shall He speak of and He will show you things to come. Work out your own* **salvation** *with fear and trembling, for it is* **God** *who works in you both to will and to do of His good pleasure, [but] prove [test carefully] all things,"* **(John 16:13, Philippians 2:12-13 & 1 Thessalonians 5:20)**

17) *"If any of you lack wisdom, let him ask of* **God** *that gives to all men liberally and upbraids not and it shall be given to him,"* **(James 1:5)**

18) *"Beloved, believe not every* **Spirit** *[who tries to guide you] but try [that is test] the* **Spirits** *[to ascertain] whether they are of* **God,** *because many false prophets [offering false forms of guidance] have gone out into the* **World,***"* **(1 John 4:10)**

Commentary

From such passages it is possible to see that, in His mercy, the **Lord** *promises to guide every single believer, no matter how aware or unaware they may be of His presence. However, this guarantee does not absolve them from such responsibilities as the need to seek* **God's** *will, to work out their own* **salvation** *and to rigorously check that their guidance emanates from the right* **Spiritual** *sources.*

Concluding exhortation

Therefore, take encouragement from **God's** repeated promises to guide His people. Be willing to ask for His guidance in prayer. However, <u>do not forget to rigorously test</u> that any prophetic guidance being given originates in the **Holy Spirit** and not from some **unclean Spirit** whose utterances mislead people to destruction.

From this **DIY homiletic Midrash** on *'Divine Guidance'* it is possible to see that a return to first century **Jewish** methods of **Bible** interpretation can still do much to open up **God's** word for today. Especially noteworthy, is the way various passages were brought together in order to emphasise a key point, along with carefully highlighted amplifications used in order to bring out the full meaning of a passage. As a side note, it is worth mentioning that modern information technology's ability to attractively format **Bible** Commentaries could greatly facilitate the growing importance of **Midrash Hermeneutics**.

Midrash can also be fun. A playful element may enter with **Parabolic Midrash** where sometimes-humorous stories are used to illustrate what is often a very serious point. This is done in order to challenge conventional thinking and to present what may be an unpalatable truth in an acceptable manner. An instance of this is the following **Parabolic Midrash,** illustrates the point that **God** will, in the end totally reject those who give themselves over to the influence of unclean **Spirit**s even though they may profess to be His people. In order to highlight the **Biblical** basis of this point the **Parabolic Midrash** will be preceded by an appropriate passage from **Scripture**.

Introductory Formula: *"Divine revelation warns"*

Scripture Reading: *"He that is unjust, let him be unjust still: and he which is filthy, let him be filthy still. For without* [the **New Jerusalem**] *are dogs, and sorcerers, and whoremongers, and murderers, and idolaters, and whosoever loves and makes a lie. Their part* [shall be] *in the lake of fire which burns with fire and brimstone: which is the second death."* **(Revelation 22:11a, 15 & 21:8c)**

A Parabolic Midrash: The Parable Of The Drunken Knight

"There was once a man who was going to be knighted by a King in a far-off country. Now this king was very stern and was known to expect the very highest standards from all of his subjects. The night before his honour the man stayed in a very luxurious five-star hotel next to the King's palace. There he fell in with bad company; he got drunk and started to boast of his greatness. So drunk did he become that he vomited all over the place – even on the expensive suit he was to wear to the palace. The next day he

woke up with a dreadful hangover and was sick a few more times. Suddenly realising that he was late for the ceremony, he brushed his hair, cleaned his suit as best he could and rushed off to the palace. There he was stopped by a stern looking guard who refused to give him entrance."
"Let me in, let me in" the man pleaded "I've got an appointment with the King. He wants to honour me, for I love him as a loyal subject."
To which comment the guard replied, "No one who really loves the King arrives late at the palace smelling of vomit."

So it is with all those **Messianic Jews** *who have received the* **Toronto Experience."**

Perhaps the last remark came as a shock; it was meant to! This is because in simple visual terms, it portrayed the tragic folly of **Messianic Jews** coming under the influence of those same **pagan Spirit**s, which helped drive **Nazism** and other **anti-Semitic** movements. Unless repented of, the long-term result of being intoxicated by such **Spirits** is exclusion from the **Messiah's** presence. **Parables** indeed can have a sting in their *'tale.'* It is hardly surprising that their use, helped get **Jesus** into a lot of trouble.

Further light can be thrown onto such deceptions as the **'Toronto Experience'** (and its subsequent **Pensacola** offshoot) by the employment of **Rez-Peshar Midrash**. Here, it is possible to resort to a *"this is that"* formula by saying *"*<u>this</u> **Toronto** phenomenon <u>is that</u> fulfilment of the warning **Paul** gave in **2 Thessalonians 2:11**. This warns **'God** *shall send them* [those who do not love the truth] *a strong delusion, that they may believe a lie.'"*

Obviously, care must be taken to distinguish between <u>a</u> fulfilment of Prophecy and the <u>final</u> fulfilment that will occur immediately prior to the **Messiah's** return. Nevertheless, **Rez-Peshar** can to some degree, show how present events fit in with the overall pattern of **Biblical** prophecy. A case in point was the **Arafat-Rabin** Peace Accord, signed in **1993**. Through **Rez-Peshar** it is possible to see that *"*<u>This</u> *event was* <u>a fulfilment</u> <u>of that</u> *Covenant with death mentioned in* **Isaiah 28:15**.*"* Lending weight to this view was **Rabin's** own assassination just over two years later. For him at least the **Palestinian** peace accord had been a *'covenant with death.'* The same could be said for all **Jews** and **Palestinians** who have been killed in subsequent **Israeli-Palestinian** disturbances.

On an even grimmer note, it is also possible to see that *"This Peace accord is that foreshadow of an even deadlier agreement that will be made by* **Israel** *with a false* **Messiah** *shortly before the outbreak of global tribulation,"* **(Daniel 9:27)**. In other words, both the **Toronto Experience** and the **Arafat-Rabin** peace accord represent the **devil's** *'dress rehearsal'* for even more extreme evils. History has clearly shown that one major obsession of the **devil** is with the destruction of **Jewish** people and **Gentile** believers alike. This is because both groups witness to the fact that the **devil** can <u>never</u> succeed in his attempt to usurp the place of the one true **God**. They also remind him of the crushing humiliation he suffered when the true **Messiah** atoned for the **World's sins** at **Calvary**. With his doom sealed, the **prince of darkness** is determined to drag as many down with him to **Hell** as possible. Any correct understanding of the many tragedies to have taken place within a **Judaic-Christian** setting can only really be gained made from a **Biblical** rather than a secular standpoint. However, such an understanding will, in this **World**, remain only partial. **Paul** acknowledged this point in **1 Corinthians 13:12a,** when he stated, *"For now we see through a glass darkly."*

Section 5: The Beauty of Midrash

One of the beauties of **Midrash** is that it allows people to find their own level in interpreting **Scripture**. It can either be very simple or very difficult. Also **Midrash** is a discipline, which embraces a number of other disciplines such as history and poetry. To successfully interpret **God's** word it is necessary to combine keen powers of analysis with imaginative storytelling and a devoted prayerfulness, with each being open to the influence of the **Holy Spirit**. Moreover, there must be a dogged willingness to accept the authority of <u>all</u> **Scripture (2 Timothy 3:16).** Also included must be a desire to follow the <u>sound</u> principles of **Bible** interpretation (as outlined in **Section 3**). One further point is that **Midrash** should enable all interested parties within the **Church** to make a <u>discerning</u> return to first century **Jewish** methods of **Bible** interpretation. In this matter, as in all others it is **Scripture** that must have the last word. However, this return to **Jewish** Methodology is something, which is both very ancient and very good. Admittedly, the past cannot be relived but it can still act as a living source, nurturing our own contemporary **Spiritual** and personal development. The past is drawn upon to influence the present. **Midrash** performs a vital task by establishing firm links between the past, present and future.

It should now be reasonably clear that **Midrash**, if wisely used not only throws greater light upon the teaching of **God's** word; but also provides a tool to see the significance of current events. Confusion is reduced as events are fitted into a wider scheme of things. **Midrash** can be used to interpret both human history and current events. Some of the laws governing human behaviour at both an individual and mass social scale are uncovered. As the writer began to discover in **November 2003,** the tools used to interpret human behaviour as recorded in **Scripture**, can also be used to interpret behaviour that has occurred outside the **Biblical** record. The discipline of **Midrash** can therefore be applied in **non-theological** subject areas like **sociology** and **psychology.** It can also provide a great deal of insight into why human organizations and societies fail (through either becoming highly destructive or totally ineffective). Admittedly, **Midrash** cannot explain every aspect of human behaviour – but it can offer a wider explanation than that provided by current theories whose basis often lies in a **secular** (non-religious) view of the **World**. **Midrash** does indeed have the potential to contribute to some major theoretical breakthroughs in the **Social Sciences.**

Midrash possesses a number of other benefits too; among these are its assistance in the understanding of doctrine and the promotion of **Spiritual** growth with its stress upon the <u>eternal</u> truthfulness of **God's** word. It is also a versatile discipline offering a whole range of perspectives to both the layperson and scholar alike. People are free to find their own level of competence in handling **Scripture**. Another advantage is that it can be adapted to different learning styles – appealing both to **auditory** (who learn through hearing) and **visual** (who learn through seeing) learners.

Moving onto a wider corporate level, the large-scale adoption of **Midrash** could help counter the many **Spiritual** deceptions that have been to rampage unchecked throughout the **Church**. On a more positive note, **Midrash** can actively buttress true doctrine, especially in relation to the more controversial such as the **Trinity. Midrash** simply confirms that all true doctrine has a solid basis in divine revelation. The myth that it represents as a strange offshoot of **Greek Philosophy** or was solely the outcome of **Church** politics would (at least amongst serious opinion), be utterly discredited. The introduction of **Midrash** could well lead to a revival of confidence in **Creed- based** doctrine. Above all, by adopting the **Midrashic** method of interpretation people would be encouraged to see for themselves who the **Messiah** is. With His **Jewish** identity thrown into sharp relief, they would then be free to make up their own minds over the validity of His claims. No high-pressure sales techniques would be needed, <u>for the truth can stand upon its own merits</u>. Indeed, such techniques are a blasphemy because they ignore the **Scripture** dictum, which states *"<u>Not</u> by might, <u>nor</u> by power, but <u>by</u> my **Spirit**, says the **Lord** of hosts."* **(Zechariah 4:6b)** If nothing else, **Midrash** can at least encourage a humble dependence upon the **Holy Spirit** to actively interpret **God's** word. **Midrash** achieves this by focusing the listener's attention upon the word itself. They are encouraged to relate to it directly at every level of their personality. **Midrash** can simultaneously engage the mind, the heart and the will.

All of the benefits already outlined are available because **Midrash** represents the means whereby divine revelation is actively accessed and interpreted. This is simply because it interprets the **Bible** in the way in which it was meant to be interpreted. Its great strength lies in the fact that it recognises that **<u>Scripture</u>** <u>is its own best interpreter</u>. The practice of **Midrash** is the equivalent of applying **Scriptural** teaching in the all-important area of **Hermeneutics.** Rarely before has a **theological** discipline, appeared more relevant; its revival, if wisely handled, could be a source of great blessing, both to **Jewish** and **Christian** communities alike.

SELECTIVE BIBLIOGRAPHY

Book List

Aaronovitch David (2009)
Voodoo Histories:
The Role of the Conspiracy Theory in Shaping Modern History
Jonathan Cape
ISBN: 978-0-224-07470-4

Alexander S. Philip – editor (1984)
Textual Sources for the Study of Judaism
Manchester University Press
ISBN: 0-7190-1498-0 (pbk)

Campbell Colin (2007)
The Easternization of the West:
A Thematic Cultural Change in the Modern Age
Paradigm Publishers
ISBN: 978-1-59451-224-7

Carson A.D & Williamson M.C.H (1988)
It Is Written; Scripture Citing Scripture
Cambridge University Press ISBN: 0-521-32347-9

Danby Herbert – editor (1954)
The Mishnah
Oxford University Press

Dockery Davis (1992)
Bible Interpretation Then And Now
Baker House ISBN: 0-8010-3010-2

Eisennman Robert & Wise Michael (1992)
The Dead Sea Scrolls Uncovered
Element ISBN: 1-85230-368-9

Ellison L. H. (1978)
Understanding a Jew
The Olive Press
ISBN: 0-904054 01-2

Epstein Isidore (1979)
Judaism
Penguin
ISBN: 0-01402-0440-7

Guthrie Donald (1990)
Hebrews: An Introduction And Commentary
IVP ISBN: 0-8028-1427-1

Fruchtenbaum G. Arnold (1994)
Israelology:
The Missing Link in Systematic Theology
Ariel ministries
ISBN: 0-914863-05-3

Horner E. Barry (2004)
Future Israel:
Why Christian Anti-Judaism Must Be Challenged
B & H Publishing Group
ISBN: 978-0-8054-4627-2

Hughes Graham (1979)
Hebrews and Hermeneutics: The Epistle To The Hebrews As A New Testament Example Of Biblical Interpretation
Cambridge University Press ISBN: 0-521-21858-6

Jessup Gordon (1976)
No strange G-d:
An outline of Jewish Life and Faith
The Olive Press
ISBN: 0-904054-X

Jr. Kaiser C. Walter (1985)
The Uses Of The Old Testament In The New
Moody Press ISBN: 0-8024-9085-9

Longnecker Richard (1975)
Biblical Exegesis In The Apostolic Period
Eerdmans ISBN: 0-8078-1560-3

Malz Steve (2009)
How the Church Lost the Way and how it can find it again
Saffron Planet
ISBN: 978-0-9562296-0-1

Moreton Cole (2010)
Is God Still An Englishman?
How We Lost Our Faith
(But Found New Soul)
Little Brown
ISBN: 978-1-4087-0180-5

Newman Israel Louis (1925)
Jewish Influence on Christian Reform Movements
Columbia University press

Oduor J. M. Reginald (1996)
To the Jew First:
The Believer's Responsibility towards Israel
Berean Publications Ltd

Phillips Melanie (2010)
The World Turned Upside Down:
The Global Battle over God, truth, and Power
Encounter Books
ISBN: 978-1-59403-375-9 486

Pink W. Arthur (1990)
Interpretation of the Scriptures
Baker House ISBN; 1-870855-01-9

Rees Laurence (2005)
Auschwitz : The Nazis & The 'Final Solution'
BBC Books
ISBN: 0-563-52117-1

Vermes G. (1973)
The Dead Sea Scrolls in English
Penguin
ISBN: 0-1402-0 551-9

Wurmbrand Richard (1975)
Christ on the Jewish Road
Hodder and Stoughton
ISBN: 0-340-19956-3

Wouk Herman (1977)
This Is My G-d
Fontana/Collins
ISBN: 0-00-613539-0

Articles

Prasch Jacob (1993)
Is The Time Appropriate To Consider Restoring The Original Jewish Hermeneutics Of The New Testament?
Tishrei Magazine Volume 1 No. 4 Summer 1993

Prasch Jacob (1994)
Midrash – A Brief Explanation
Moriel Paper and Moriel Tapes on The Same Theme
Issued On Various Dates During The 1993-1996 Period

Sheehan Bob (1994)
The Sufficiency Of Scripture
Reformation Today Magazine July/August 1994 Issue 140

Reference Works

Purdy C. Alexander (1955)
The Epistle to the Hebrews;
The Interpreter's Bible, Volume 11
Abingdon Press (H/B) Ref: D-0.3 Bib

Encyclopaedia Judaica (1971)
Volumes 8 and 11
Keter Publishing
Ref: 296.03 Eni 19

Sources for the Scriptural passages include various Concordances and the writer's own memory

Media Sources

Small Peter (2007)
Rabbi Ascherman, Human-Rights Activist
Sunday Times Magazine, 30th December 2007
Times Newspapers Ltd

Sunday Today:
A look at the ethical and religious issues of the week
Radio 4,
Sunday, 6th June 1999

Various Sources

1) The writer's late father who (in a succession of private conversations) taught him to love the Jewish people and to see that G-d had a purpose for them.
2) Numerous speakers, tape recordings and items of literature taken from those engaged in Christian work amongst the Jews – some dating back to the mid-1970s
3) Sources already listed in the selective bibliography of *'The Leeds Liturgy'*

OTHER TITLES BY THE AUTHOR

NOTICE

For information on the ordering and pricing of these titles please visit
http://stores.lulu.com/rebuildchristianity or
http://stores.lulu.com/store.php?fAcctID=976144

Soft cover versions of these titles should be available through Amazon and other International Distributors.

In the event of any difficulty with these *'links'* please search using the *'Book Title' and* the name *'Raymond Creed.'* Doing this should access a relevant site.

THE 52 ATTRIBUTES OF G-D

'The 52 Attributes of God' explores God's unique character. It uses ancient Jewish methods of bible interpretation (*'Midrash'*) along with prayerful meditations, proverbial sayings and simple summaries. Each chapter combines both analytical with devotional material and readers are encouraged to progress at their own pace. *'The 52 Attributes of God'* is readily accessible for both private and group use and employs a stimulating variety of questions to aid reflection and to encourage practical application. It shows how all 52 of the divine attributes were displayed during Christ's death and it helps rebuild Christianity by using *'Midrash'* to provide a clearer picture of God's nature.

Great care is taken to answer such questions as: -
1) Who is God?
2) What is He like?
3) How did He react to the death of His Son Jesus?
4) How does He react to the corruption found within much of today's Church?
5) To what extent can we become like God?

'The 52 Attributes of God' should prove particularly useful to religious ministers (of all denominational backgrounds), local church elders, Christian teachers, evangelists and theological students. The Messianic Jewish community and those wishing to delve deeper into theology would especially benefit. Any public or academic library with a theological section will find it a rich resource. It should also be of assistance to those confused or troubled by beguiling *'spiritualities'* which alluringly offer the chance to become divine.

This book ends by warning that those choosing to ignore the clear distinction between God and Man (by presuming they have a right to become mini-gods) often end up behaving like devils.

To purchase a download, hard or soft cover edition please visit: -

http://stores.lulu.com/rebuildchristianity or

http://stores.lulu.com/store.php?fAcctID=976144

Soft cover editions may also be available through Amazon and other International Distributors.

THE LEEDS LITURGY

The Leeds Liturgy' encourages Christians to worship God *"in spirit and in truth"* (John 4:24). In terms of doctrine, it aspires to be the truest and most accurate book outside of scripture. Its pages contain *'The Leeds Creed'* which is the most comprehensive creedal *'Statement of Faith'* in Christianity to date, (Acts 20:27). This *'statement'* integrates bible-based insights from every Christian Tradition and provides a comprehensive summary of those doctrines needed for salvation and for effective Christian living. Also included are revised versions of the Apostles, Nicene and Athanasian Creeds.

'The Leeds Liturgy' aims to: -
1) Provide a legacy of truth for present and future believers
2) Testify to the one true Gospel that *"Jesus Christ came into the world to save sinners,"* (I Timothy 1:15b)
3) Portray doctrine in a fresh, interactive and understandable way
4) Promote an exuberant style of worship
5) Declare the *'whole counsel [full teaching] of God'* to a Church that currently seems to value everything else but the teaching of Scripture
6) Enable believers (largely due to its provision of sound doctrinal teaching) to better withstand persecution and hardship
7) Bring Jew and Gentile together in joint worship of the one true God of Israel
8) Nurture the community life of Messianic Jewish and Christian groups
9) Offer a distinctive way of presenting timeless truths to a sinful world
10) Enable believers to interact with bible teaching (either individually or in a group setting)

'The Leeds Liturgy' proclaims the Gospel by pointing to Christ as the only means whereby eternal life is received. His full deity and full humanity are equally emphasised – as is the Trinitarian relationship between Himself, His Father and the Holy Spirit. Christians are encouraged to relate to these Persons through the material provided in this resource. It attempts to be a vehicle with the innate capacity to be used by the Holy Spirit, who eagerly wants to lead Christians into all truth, (John 16:13a). It highlights the fact that, to place our faith in God, we must first lose faith in ourselves.

'*The Leeds Liturgy*' closes with two articles exploring the biblical roots of Liturgies and Creeds. These could be of special interest to students working in the field of liturgical studies. Its successor volume, '*Facing the Unthinkable*' provides a dramatic anticipation of how Israel will recognize the true messiah during a period of great affliction.

To purchase a download, hard or soft cover edition please visit: -

http://stores.lulu.com/rebuildchristianity or

http://stores.lulu.com/store.php?fAcctID=976144

Soft cover versions may also be available through Amazon and other International Distributors.

THE PHANTOM CONFLICT

'The Phantom Conflict' endeavours to rebuild Christianity by showing how a balanced emphasis between divine holiness and divine love is a prerequisite for healthy Christian living. The problem of Christian idolatry is also tackled.

'The Phantom Conflict' addresses the following questions: -
1) How does divine holiness relate to divine love?
2) How is it possible to avoid incorrect views of G-d?
3) How is it possible to avoid idolatry?

'The Phantom Conflict,' assumes that correct ideas of G-d are a vital precondition to spiritual fruitfulness. It argues that to exaggerate divine holiness at the expense of divine love (or vice-versa) produces a warped and ineffective version of Christianity. At one extreme, it becomes a religion of fear and at the other a religion of flippancy. Both deviations harm their adherents and discredit the gospel.

This book should prove particularly useful to religious ministers (of all denominational backgrounds), local church elders, Christian teachers, evangelists and theological students. The Messianic Jewish community and those wishing to delve deeper into theology would also benefit.

'The Phantom Conflict' serves as a practical and interactive teaching tool, being divided into easily accessible sections, all undergirded by ancient Jewish methods of bible interpretation ('Midrash'). It may be regarded as an independent work or as a successor volume to 'The 52 Attributes of G-d.'

To purchase a download, hard or soft cover edition please visit: -

http://stores.lulu.com/rebuildchristianity or

http://stores.lulu.com/store.php?fAcctID=976144

Soft cover editions may also be available through Amazon and other International Distributors.

TITLES IN PREPARATION

ANCIENT HATRED

Ancient Hatred forms the first part of this creative and dramatic work. It consists of Four Acts centred on the theme of human rebellion against God. Its destructive consequences, along with Humanity's increased vulnerability to satanic deception, are looked at in-depth. A definite sequential relationship is embedded within that initial rebellion against God, as shown here: -

Humanity's rebellion against God
⇓
Domination by sinful passions
⇓
The production of long-lasting hatreds
⇓
Faithlessness in the Church
⇓
Vulnerability to satanic deception
⇓
The development of a *'New World Order'* representing that deception
⇓
The rise of a false Messiah to head that *'Order'*
⇓
The persecution of Jewish and Christian dissenters
⇓
Bitterly destructive consequences
⇓
The near destruction of Humanity

Readers will quickly gather from **Ancient Hatred** that the emphasis is very much upon the awful consequences of human sin. Humanity descends into its own man-made Hell whilst the Church degenerates into a willing tool of the anti-Christ. Although shards of light emerge in meditations like *'The Spirit Calls'* it is the dark side of life which comes to the fore. God is portrayed as a wrathful judge – allowing people to experience the bitter consequences of their rebellion against Him. The focus centres upon Man's alienation from God – an alienation often hidden under the guise of religion. Covered in meditations like *'Lament for a Lost Friend'* and *'My Lady'* is the cost apostasy incurs in terms of broken relationships, moral scandal and emotional distress. Such pieces confirm I am is approaching this problem – not as some *'ivory tower'* critic of the Church but as an active participant who has been *'in the thick of it.'* I know what it's like to have been distressed by some of the situations described in this book. I want to convey to future generation what it was like to have lived through a period of mass apostasy and growing social madness.

ANCIENT LOVE

Ancient Love shifts emphatically from human rebellion to divine redemption – with the person and work of Jesus being the central theme. Highlighted is the way Christ's death upon the cross is the only answer to human sinfulness. Quite deliberately, a contrast is drawn between the ancient hatreds of humanity and the ancient (or eternal) love of God. God's love is open to anyone to receive it, should they so choose (with God's help) to believe that the Lord Jesus Christ is their only saviour from sin. Embedded within God's divine redemption is the following causal relationship: -

God's everlasting, passionate love
⇓
A passion to create
⇓
The creation of the universe
⇓
The giving of freewill to both angels and people
⇓
The foundation of Israel
⇓
The redemptive sacrifice of Jesus
⇓
The foundation of the Church
⇓
The restoration of the Jewish people
⇓
The return of Jesus to rescue Humanity from extinction
⇓
The judgement and forcible removal of evil
⇓
The installation of God's perfect kingdom on earth

The emphasis is upon the many wonderful results of salvation (although the awful consequences of rejecting that salvation are not ignored). Hardly surprisingly, there are many worship pieces in **Ancient Love** Each one encourages the believer to participate in the loving fellowship already existing between all three Persons of the divine Trinity.

Already present in draft form, both parts of *'Ancient Passions'* are scheduled for release in late 2019 or early 2020.

NOTES

www.ingramcontent.com/pod-product-compliance
Lightning Source LLC
Chambersburg PA
CBHW051808040426
42446CB00007B/571